FROM RUINS TO REBUILDING

FROM RUINS TO REBUILDING

Lessons from the Book of Nehemiah

BURLISS PARKER

Pleasant Word
A Division of WINEPRESS PUBLISHING

Pleasant Word (a division of WinePress Publishing, PO Box 428, Enumclaw, WA 98022) functions only as book publisher. As such, the ultimate design, content, editorial accuracy, and views expressed or implied in this work are those of the author.

All Greek word meanings are from *Thayers Greek-English Lexicon of the New Testament*. Baker Book House: Grand Rapids, Michigan.

All Hebrew meanings are from *Gesenius–Hebrew-Chaldee Lexicon to the Old Testament*. Baker Book House: Grand Rapids, Michigan.

Strong's Exhaustive Concordance. Baker Book House: Grand Rapids, Michigan.

ISBN 13: 978-1-4141-1194-0
ISBN 10: 1-4141-1194-0
Library of Congress Catalog Card Number: 2008901508

CONTENTS

ACKNOWLEDGMENTS

I WOULD LIKE to take this opportunity to thank my wife, Dawn, for encouraging me to write the book and my daughter, Brittany (it is one of her favorite sermons). Also, a big thank you to Buffy Smith for her typing skills and time. And a thank you to Reverend Bill Loudermilk, who, after hearing this message, said, "That needs to be a book." Thank you, Bill.

INTRODUCTION

FROM RUINS TO *Rebuilding* is based on lessons from the book of Nehemiah and can be applied to any area of your life where the enemy, Satan, has attacked and caused havoc or you have experienced an unexpected twist or turn. Maybe it is not a simple twist or turn, but a downright catastrophe. What was once a peaceful existence is now filled with confusion and the endless search for answers. Your mind is filled with questions such as, *Why did this happen?* or, *Where was God when I needed Him?*

Perhaps your spouse has been unfaithful to you, but you have determined to stay together and work through the problems and keep your marriage together. Or maybe your spouse left you and now you are attempting to pick up the pieces of your life. You are trying to raise the children, pay the bills and come up with a plan of what to do next. Or it could be that a poor business decision by you or your business partner has collapsed your company and you are now filing bankruptcy.

Maybe you are recovering from being hurt during a difficult church situation. You still may be attending the church, but you slip in and out of the church doors, silently suffering. You might have left the church and are now attending another. Or perhaps you are at the other end of the spectrum and are a wounded pastor or a church leader.

It could be that you have been involved in an abusive relationship from which you are now trying to recover and heal. Or maybe you are living with a broken heart because of the sudden death of a loved one or are suffering from the loss of a close friendship.

It could even be that God has given you a vision or a promise and now it seems as if all has been ripped away from you. You feel as if you are now living in the shadows of what used to be.

If any of the above situations apply to you, *From Ruins to Rebuilding* can guide you through the healing process and the journey of reconstructing your life. As we delve into the book of Nehemiah and take a closer look at these issues, we will follow the lessons of rebuilding that are found in God's Word.

Chapter 1

STEP OUT OF THE RUINS

They said to me, "The survivors who are left from the captivity in the province are there in great distress and reproach. The wall of Jerusalem is also broken down, and its gates are burned with fire."

—Neh. 1:3

THE WORD "SURVIVOR" in Hebrew means "to be left behind to remain; to be left a remnant." If you are a survivor, you are the one who is left behind to pick up the pieces after the enemy has attacked. You try to hold on to what was left of your life and make sense of what has happened in the situation. These wounds can come from a variety of sources: a broken marriage, a failed business, an unfortunate situation at church, an abusive relationship, the loss of a loved one, the loss of a friendship. In this chapter, we will examine each of these types of wounds and begin to look at the lessons of rebuilding that are found in the book of Nehemiah.

Wounds from a Broken Marriage

If a crisis has occurred in the area of marriage, you may find yourself attempting to bring stability to your home and explain to your children the problem (such as why dad or mom has left). The responsibility for the entire household now falls on your shoulders. You are riding a roller coaster of emotions. Within a matter of moments, you find yourself going from anger to disbelief to depression to confusion.

You may be angry at yourself for not seeing the signs of trouble—the "working late" at the office, the business trips that seem odd but are never questioned, the unfamiliar cell phone numbers and emails. You find it hard to believe that this is happening to you. Weren't you a good enough wife or husband? You did as God had instructed in His Word. You were faithful in giving yourself to the success of the marriage, but now it has fallen apart and the relationship is in serious trouble. You thought your marriage was strong and indestructible, but the news of the affair or the pornography you found is more than you can handle.

Allow me to relate a recent story told to me by a pastor friend. His small church was struggling and needed help in many areas. A family came in one Sunday to visit the church. On a follow up visit, he discovered that the couple was musically gifted. In a short time, they were leading the praise and worship, and the church started growing.

One Sunday morning, the wife called and said that she and her husband would not be returning to the church. My friend was baffled and asked why. The woman said that her husband's addiction to pornography had destroyed their marriage. She had tried to keep it hidden, but she could not take it anymore. Her final words were, "We will be divorcing."

There was a time when it was primarily the man who left his wife and family in these scenarios. Unfortunately, we have witnessed an increasing number of women leaving the relationship and family. The husbands are the ones left picking up the pieces and raising the children.

I know of one woman who had been married for more than 15 years. Her husband came home one day to find that she had left him and their three children. It was later discovered that she was having an affair. Not only did she divorce her husband, but she also reneged on their bills, forcing her husband into bankruptcy. To this day, the children harbor bitterness toward their mother for what she did to the family.

Wounds from a Failed Business

Crises can also occur in business relationships. Perhaps all was going well in a business venture or partnership that you began. New contracts were coming in. You were adding extra office space, hiring new employees and building a large warehouse.

Then there was a slump in sales, or the market dropped, or the economy slowed. Buyers called and canceled their orders—the slowdown hit them as well. They could no longer pay their bills. You still owe money on the buildings that were completed. The merchandise that fills your warehouses is not wanted, so it just sits. What once began as a promising business venture or new partnership has turned into a disaster. The company that you poured your life and money into is now gone.

Maybe you were in business with someone whom you thought you could trust, but then found out that he or she had been embezzling funds from the company accounts or abusing his or her privileges. Now the business is in financial ruin. You are trying to make good on the promises that were made or the contracts that were signed, but the task seems impossible. You might have suspected something was not quite right, but you were so busy holding up your end of the company that there was no time to investigate your suspicions. Instead of a having great success in your business, you are now filing for bankruptcy.

Sometimes the problem occurs because believers go into partnership with non-believers. Second Corinthians 6:14 reads, "Do not be unequally yoked together with unbelievers. For what fellowship has righteousness with lawlessness? And what communion has light with darkness." Whether it is marriage or business, the Bible clearly warns Christians not to be connected with non-believers if at all possible. The accounts of broken lives by those who have violated this principle are too numerous to tell. Let's face it—it's hard enough at times working with believers!

Wounds from a Church

Anyone who has attended a church for any length of time has undoubtedly been hurt by someone in the church at some time. I have yet to meet someone who has not been deeply wounded in his or her Christian journey.

The wounds might have come from church leaders, pastors, elders, board members or teachers. For instance, many times people of a congregation are asked to embrace the vision of the leader. Some are even pressured by the pastor and church leaders to the point that if they do not agree, they will be forced to leave the church! These leaders fail to remember that the vision of a church is not more important than the people. Jesus died for people, not visions.

Others are hurt because of a conflict with a brother or sister in the Lord. Things are said and done that are unfair, inaccurate and unkind. Instead of resolving the issue, it blows up into a bigger mess, and they end up leaving the church.

I am amazed at the number of hurting people I come into contact with on a daily basis at my church. These people have come to our church looking for a safe haven to nurse their wounds and be healed. Usually, these wounded Christians fall into one of two categories: (1) the walking wounded, or (2) the church abandoners.

1. The Walking Wounded

There are some individuals who come to church every Sunday carrying their hurt and pain in with them. Worse yet, these walking wounded are still hurting when they leave. Those in the church fail to help them address the pain in their life, or, if they do address it, often simply gloss over it without providing them with any real answers for dealing with the issue. Many times, pastors and leaders are so busy with other areas of ministry that these needs are not addressed. A typical pastor does not have the amount of time needed to counsel and minister properly. So, many times, the needs of these hurting believers are neglected.

2. The Church Abandoners

The second category of wounded Christians are those who have left a particular church and vow that they will never darken its doors again. They may go from church to church, but never find a place to settle. They still love God, read their Bible and pray at home, but they tell themselves that they will never trust a pastor, elder or church person again. They try to heal their own wounds and find their own answers, but this is not always successful.

Hurting believers who are no longer attending a church on a regular basis will create their own standard of a Christian walk. They will devise their own convictions to pacify any sense of guilt they may feel for not obeying God's Word and use an endless number of excuses for the current state of their spiritual decline. They may develop a sense of spiritual pride that tells them that they are just as close to God as they were when they were regularly attending church. Hebrews 10:25 tells us, "Not forsaking the assembling of ourselves together, as is the manner of some, but exhorting one another, and so much more as you see the day approaching." These believers can make all the excuses they want, but the Word of God is clear: They need to belong to a church for spiritual health, healing and growth. A complete healing must take place for these believers to get back on track in their walk with God.

Pastors often find it very difficult to gain the trust of individuals who have been hurt by the church. The pastor must prove that he or she has no hidden agenda other than their healing. If the pastor's motive is to get another family or tither into church and the hurt is ignored, these wounded Christians will see this and will leave. If, however, the pastor is genuinely concerned for their healing, they will often allow the pastor into their lives, and the healing process can begin. When this occurs, it is exciting to watch these saints believe God again.

In our church, when we have helped people begin and complete the healing process, we have also learned to let them go. Some churches seem to be the healing station for the wounded. Once that has been done, some stay while others move on.

The Wounded Church Leader

Another category of wounded Christian is the wounded church leader. Often, the leader brings this pain on himself or herself. In other instances, the leader is wounded by those in his or her church.

Church Leaders Who Bring Pain on Themselves

One way that leaders bring pain on themselves is through moral failure. I have been serving the Lord for more than 25 years. During that time, I have had the opportunity to serve as a pastor, district superintendent, regional board member, and on our denomination's mission board. Having served in these offices, I have had the unfortunate experience of being called to an emergency board meeting because of the moral failure of a pastor.

In one such meeting, the pastor confessed that he was having an affair with a woman in the congregation. The relationship had been discovered when he called her to find out when and where they would be meeting. She picked up the phone on the last ring, not realizing that the answering machine in the basement had engaged and was recording the entire conversation.

Once behind closed doors, we listened to the story of how the affair began. The pastor told us of the planned rendezvous and the suspicions that his wife had but could not put her finger on. As always, once Satan had trapped him and the woman, the secret was revealed and everything began to fall apart.

A second way that pastors or leaders hurt themselves is through their lack of leadership ability. Pastors can have a vision, but they must also have the ability to follow through on that vision or gather people around them who can. The stress of failing, or a failed vision, will cause leaders to think irrationally. For instance, they might start covering over the financial problems by inflating income or attendance numbers. They may look for ways to rid themselves of the stress—often by turning to the way of the world instead of to God.

A third way that pastors hurt themselves is by setting themselves up as dictators. They demand their congregation's allegiance to themselves in the name of the Lord. Often, these types of leaders manipulate and lie to those following them so that they can get their own way. They may even cover over improper relationships or questionable financial practices by claiming that what they are doing is for the ministry. Once the people in the church begin to see through this conduct and begin questioning the leader's motives, the pastor may fight back and tell the people that they did not hear from God. Often, they are asked to submit or leave.

I have never met a leader who has had a failure of any kind who began the ministry with the idea of having an affair, taking money, believing that their leadership skills were inadequate, or determining to set themselves up as dictators. The pressure they experience in the ministry or mission field can often lead to their failures.

Church Leaders Who Are Wounded by Those in the Church

My heart goes out to those leaders who have been wounded by people in their congregations, as they have simply tried to obey God's calling in their lives and shepherd the flock God has given them. Whether they are pastoring a church or are denominational leaders, there are and always will be wolves in sheep's clothing. Matthew 7:15-16 says, "Beware of false prophets, who come to you in sheep's clothing, but inwardly they are ravenous wolves…you will know them by their fruits." Examining this verse will give us insights into the motives of some of the people who are in our churches.

"Beware of false prophets …"

"False prophets" are those who act the part of a divinely inspired prophet. They utter falsehoods under the name of the Lord. They may be people who are already in the church. They always have a "word from God" for the leader and his or her family. Pastors should especially beware if this is the fourth church they have been to in the last two years—they probably have been asked to leave every other place they have been. The pastor should find out the church these individuals came from and call that pastor. It may save them a lot of heartache.

We pastored our first church in Ohio. One day, I received a phone call from a pastor in the town next to us who told me of a woman and her three sons who had just left his church. He said that she had been to every church in their town and had been asked to leave each church after only a few months. The trouble and pain that her family left in its wake was heartbreaking to hear.

This pastor called to warn me of this family. A few weeks later, the woman and her sons arrived at our church. I did not know who they were until I heard the woman's name. Immediately, I began to confront her with what I was told. She thought I was crazy, but I wanted to protect the sheep God had given to me. She told me she was a prophetess, but that the pastors of the churches she had attended would not listen to her. She gave me a few examples of what she had said. It was destructive and unbiblical. I asked her to leave and not come back.

The woman and her family went to another church. So I called the pastor and told him what I had done and warned him of her conduct. Unfortunately, he rejected my warning. In three months' time, she had split his church by getting the people in his congregation to focus on his faults (which is not hard to do, because pastors *are* human). After sowing the seeds of discontent, the pastor's congregation turned on him. The result was devastating.

Another time, I went to speak at a church that had previously had a man come and conduct a prophecy seminar. A woman in the congregation related this story to me. The man was teaching them how to be prophets. At one of the breaks in the seminar, she overheard one of the participants ask the instructor, "What if I do not have a prophecy for someone who has asked me to give one?" His response was, "If you do not have anything to say, just make something up. They will never know anyway."

This is the conduct of a false prophet. I realize that there are those who legitimately operate in these gifts. But whatever is spoken must be weighed against the Word of God, and only time will tell the accuracy of what was said.

"Who Come To You In Sheep's Clothing ..."

"Sheep's clothing" means "a lamb-like exterior." On the outside, these false prophets appear to be living a godly life. They know what to say and how to act, "but inwardly they are ravenous wolves." "Inwardly" is the place where God sees. He looks upon their motives—the plans that have been formed and what they believe in their secret places. These plans may be hidden from others, but not from God. Eventually, what is inside comes out.

"But inwardly they are ravenous wolves"

A "ravenous wolf" is a robber, or person who extorts. They come in and rob a church's vision, strength, blessing, joy and purpose. If allowed, they will take everything that God has promised. Oftentimes, churches and pastors are so desperate to increase their attendance that they do not question people about where they have been and why they are at the church. Wolves are cruel, greedy and destructive. They do not come in to help the church but are sent by Satan to destroy it.

We have always had a 90-day rule in the churches we have pastored. This allows time for us to get to know the people that have come in and for them to get to know us. They get to know our vision and direction and determine whether or not they want to join us.

Remember that wolves run in packs. They either come in as a pack, or a leader arises and gathers a pack around himself or herself. How many times have you heard, "I am not the only one who feels this way"? Wolves run in packs and attack in packs.

These wolves can be on your staff, council or church board, or they can be people in the pew. I have heard of accounts of pastors going on vacation, only to return and find that the board had a meeting while they were gone. On their return, they are notified that they are no longer wanted and have 30 days to move out of the church and get a new job.

Church Leaders Who Are Wounded by Those Over Them

Having served as a district superintendent, I know how difficult it is to make decisions concerning pastors and churches. Sometimes this leads to bad feelings or wounding of the church leader and the congregation. In some cases, pastors and churches remove themselves from denominational covering because they have been hurt by the actions of the leaders of the denomination.

There are advantages and disadvantages of being in a denomination. The advantages are:

1. There is accountability for the senior pastor and leadership of a church. The people in the congregation have someone to turn to who is over the leaders of the congregation if they believe things are getting off track.
2. The church can quickly replace the leadership. When a pastor or lead elder steps down, there is a pool of likeminded individuals who can be called on to fill the leadership positions.
3. The church can accomplish more. Being in a fellowship of churches allows individual churches to accomplish more because they are part of a group. The pooling of resources can support missionary families and men's, women's, youth, children's and other ministries.

An independent church may not have access to these advantages. However, they have other benefits:

1. There is no denomination or group telling the church what to believe or to interfere with its vision or direction it is going.

2. The finances of the church can be directed to the ministries and projects of its choosing.
3. There are no leaders who have influence on the church's future.

Having served in both roles, I can honestly say neither is better than the other. It is a matter of how God is directing each leader and congregation.

To return to my original point, church leaders can be wounded by those over them. Often, the situation involves dealing with a pastor who is greatly loved by the members of his congregation, and even though there was disciplinary action taken because of a moral failure, the congregation wants him to remain the pastor. Unless the failure was sexual in nature, it is unlikely that the denomination will allow the pastor to stay. In most cases, having the pastor remain as a leader is simply not acceptable. If this results in the church pulling out of the denomination, it can leave a bad taste in the mouths of the congregants for organized religion.

Sometimes a church leader will make decisions that will impact the future of pastors to advance up the organizational ladder. Unfortunately, all too often it is not what the pastor knows, but who he or she knows. This scenario is played out behind closed doors. Men and women who are qualified and called to go to the next level of leadership are denied opportunities to advance because they are not in the right circle. Worse yet, those who are promoted have fewer qualifications. Within a short time on the job, their inability to lead becomes apparent, yet they are left in those positions because the leadership will not recognize its mistake and correct it. The problem with this is that not only does the person in the office suffer, but so do the people he or she is overseeing. As a result, many men and women become frustrated with the politics or denominational leadership and leave for independent church positions (or leave ministry altogether).

James 3:6 reads, "The tongue…sets on fire the course of nature, and it is set on fire by hell." To "set something on fire" means to destroy or to operate destructively. "The course of nature" means the wheel of life. In other words, the tongue can destroy someone else's life by changing the course that had been set for him or her by God. James tells us that this kind of destructiveness is from hell, or is influenced by hell.

Yes, God calls people to rise to the next level of leadership that He has prepared for them. But the powers that are in charge make decisions that actually change the course of those individuals' lives. This leaves them feeling baffled as to what happened. They begin to doubt their ability to hear from God.

Perhaps the person is a strong and outspoken leader, or maybe that individual spoke his or her mind to a leader over him or her. Then, while in a council meeting, the board determines that they do not want such boldness in leadership. Not only is the person shattered because of the outcome of their decision, but something else has happened: the leader has joined the ranks of the "functioning wounded." The leader still has to go about his or her daily duties, listening to the struggles of others while he or she ties to cope with his or her own disappointment. It is very difficult to care for and reach out to others in this state of mind, but the leader must carry on.

The truth for those in leadership positions is that regardless of whether the wounds came from people in the church or from a leader over them, they must deal with the issue and receive healing from the events that have happened. If not, the leaders will just carry these wounds with them from church to church or ministry to ministry.

Wounds from an Abusive Relationship

Abusive relationships fall into many categories. We have already discussed abusive church leaders, so we will move on and cover two other types of abuse: (1) verbal abuse and (2) physical abuse.

Verbal Abuse

As we discussed, James 3:6 states, "The tongue…sets on fire the course of nature." Verbal abuse can change the course of a person's outcome in life. A child or an adult who has been told that he or she is dumb or stupid has a mountain to climb in life if they are going to accomplish anything in life. The same is true for the person who has been told that he or she is unattractive and that no one would want them.

Physical Abuse

Physical abuse in families, like verbal abuse, often occurs behind closed doors. Only the spouse and children know what is happening. In one church we pastored, a lady called me to make an appointment, saying that it was urgent. When she entered my office, she began to cry uncontrollably. After praying and waiting for her to calm down, she began to tell me of her husband's violent temper. I was shocked! He was the quietest man in the church. A few weeks later, she called and asked me to come to her house as quickly as possible. Before I arrived, the man had flipped over the furniture in the living room and torn pictures off the wall. The place was a mess.

I came to realize that the man was using his anger to control and intimidate his family into submission. However, as the children grew older and left home, they refused to let his outbursts affect them. Of course, that made him even madder. Now the children only come around when necessary. They have little use for their father.

In many situations, the victim will stand up to the abuser and confront the person with an ultimatum that if the abuse does not stop, he or she will leave or turn the abuser over to the authorities. This works for a while, but most often the person slips back to his or her old ways. However, once the final decision has been made to bring the abuse to an end, the next challenge for the victim will be to recover from the physical, mental and emotional scars. The goal for the person is now to rebuild his or her life. The hardest part of that journey is to somehow learn to trust people again.

Wounds from the Loss of a Loved One

The death of a loved one is one of the most difficult and heartbreaking events you will experience in life. This is true regardless of whether it is a sudden death or you have witnessed the loved one's gradual decline and suffering from a disease. I remember the morning I received the phone call that my dad had passed away. We had just been with him a few days before while celebrating my parent's thirty-fifth wedding anniversary. Dad was laughing, joking and enjoying the moment. He appeared to be perfectly normal. Then the call came from out of nowhere that he was dead. He had suffered a heart attack at age 61.

Within a three-year period, my grandmother, mother and mother-in-law had died. Grief overload! It took me more than a year to adjust to the void that was left in my life. What a reality check! We all know that people do not live forever. But when it actually happens, it can cause you to rethink what is important in life.

The sudden death of a spouse, child or other loved one is devastating—especially if he or she was a young man or woman whose life was still ahead of him or her. This kind of loss is hard to comprehend. You can struggle with how God could have allowed such a tragedy to take place. Where was He? What was the loved one's spiritual condition at the time of death?

Maybe you have been praying for someone who is dying, asking God to heal them. You have been trusting God to intervene on that person's behalf and believing in Him for a miraculous healing. But to your disappointment, the word comes that the person has passed away. Why did God not answer your prayer? You trusted, you believed, and your faith was engaged with all of the spiritual strength you could muster. You did everything the Bible instructed you to do when believing God for a miracle. But instead, you found yourself standing next to a casket.

Not only are you dealing with the devastating loss of a loved one, but you are also dealing with the death of a vision. The plans you made for the future will now not take place. I know that my wife and I have made many plans for our future—the direction of our ministry, where we would like to be five years from now, the hope we have and how we think we are going to get there. The death of either one of us would mean a death of the vision, for when the person you are making plans with dies, so does your future with him or her. Yet with time and healing, there will again be a new vision and new hopes.

Wounds from the Loss of a Friendship

The final topic I would like to address before we move on is the wounds suffered from the loss of a friendship. Suffering the loss of a close friendship is extremely difficult. The parting of ways could have been as simple as you deciding to do something different and not including your friend, and he or she took that personally. Your friend may have demanded that you choose a side in the midst of a church split or a relationship that he or she was involved in. Your friend wanted your opinion and you gave it, but it was not what they wanted to hear. Now, perhaps someone you had been friends with for years won't even speak to you. You have tried to speak to the person in an effort to restore your friendship, but they will not even acknowledge your efforts.

The Function of Walls

In each of these scenarios, you will most likely be tempted to blame God or to be angry at Him for allowing these things to happen to you. Why didn't He prevent it? Why didn't He stop this from happening? Why did He let it go this far? Where was His protection? Where was His promise? After the initial shock of what has happened has passed, you will then be faced with the decision of either living in the ruins of what has taken place or gathering the strength to change your circumstances and walk through the process of healing.

In the book of Nehemiah, the children of Israel were faced with the same dilemma. In 586 B.C., the Babylonian king Nebuchadnezzar marched his armies to the city of Jerusalem. He destroyed the city, pillaged the Temple of God, burned the gates and tore down the walls of the city. The people were led away, which began the period known as "the Babylonian captivity." Then, after a time, a remnant of the Israelites were allowed to return to the city of Jerusalem. One of these returning Israelites, a man named Nehemiah, was given an assignment from God to rebuild the walls and hang the gates.

Walls have only two functions: to keep something out or to keep something in. Both are viewed as ways of protecting. Such walls can be placed into three categories:

1. *Literal walls.* The first category is the literal wall, such as the one Nehemiah was assigned by God to rebuild around the city of Jerusalem. The original walls were built to keep out the Israelites' enemies,

such as the Babylonians. But Nebuchadnezzar set up camp and waited for the people of the city to run out of supplies. The walls that were built to protect them then became a prison. There was no choice for them then but to open the gates and surrender. They had to do this or die.

2. *Spiritual walls.* The second category involves the spiritual significance of building walls. The above example of Nebuchadnezzar setting up camp outside of Jerusalem is a great example of how Satan works out his plans against us. He camps outside of our lives and waits for an opening so he can enter. There may not be a great assault on the wall of protection around us, yet he sits outside, tempting and drawing us to open the gates and drop our guard. Once this is done, he will enter into our lives, seizing the opportunity that we have given him. Then the destruction begins. Just like Nebuchadnezzar, Satan will destroy, if possible, the very thing that kept him out. He will destroy the walls and burn the gates of our lives.

3. *Mental and emotional walls.* The third category concerns the mental and emotional walls that we build to protect ourselves. These walls are meant to keep people out, or at least at a distance. There are reasons why we build such walls. Sometimes it is because we have been deeply hurt and need to protect ourselves from more pain. We want to prevent it from happening again as much as it is in our power to do so. Other times, we put up mental

> and emotional walls because close relationships make us feel uncomfortable. We lack the skills or ability to function in a normal relationship or in society.

We all have a protective mechanism that will engage if we sense the need to protect ourselves. The key is to put up the wall as needed and lower it when it is not needed. The wall goes up to stop the enemy, stop the hurt, or to protect ourselves. But if we do not learn to lower the wall or open the gates, we may be keeping out what God wants to do in our lives. We may be keeping out the love of our family who needs access to our heart.

The Decision: Rebuild the Walls or Live in the Ruins

By the time Nehemiah arrived in Jerusalem, 142 years had passed since Nebuchadnezzar's armies destroyed the city. During that time, the Israelites who had returned had chosen to live in the ruins of the broken walls and burned gates instead of taking it upon themselves to rebuild them. The situation had become their reality and a normal part of their lives. They went about their daily routines. They married, raised children and grandchildren, and buried those who had died, all the while living in the shadow of the destroyed walls. This went on to the third and fourth generations.

There are people all around us who have experienced wounds and are now simply existing in the ruins of what has happened. These people are found in our families, in our place of employment, and in our churches. They have no desire or emotional strength to change their circumstances.

Think of the people you know who are living in the brokenness of what has happened to them. They are accepting the ruins of what has happened as normal. It is now a part of their everyday life. They lack the emotional and physical strength to move from the mindset of living in the ruins to rebuilding the walls that protect their lives from the attacks of the enemy.

Even though walls are simple, they provide a very valuable function. This is why Nehemiah's mandate from God was to rebuild the walls and replace the gates. In the same way, God does not want you living in the ruins of what has happened in your life and believing that brokenness is normal. *It is not normal.* Nor is it where God wants you to remain.

Naturally, after a traumatic event, there will be a season of depression and closing up your spirit emotionally. Yes, you have been deeply hurt. But God does not want you living in the ruins of past hurts or simply adapting to your circumstances and allowing them to become the environment that rules your life. He wants to bring you out of the ruins, help you rebuild your life under His direction, and heal the pain. He desires to come into your life and rebuild it. Only He can take the pieces of what has happened, turn it around, and make you whole again.

You may need to get professional counseling to help you sort through what has happened and assist you in setting new priorities. You will need to immerse yourself in prayer and the Word, bring stability to your home and children, hang around people who support you and give you strength, and get up and go to work everyday so you can provide for your family and pay the bills. It will be difficult, but if you trust in God, He can lead you through the healing process and begin to rebuild the walls of your life.

It is time for a new vision with a new hope, a new promise and a new purpose. But if you look at your circumstances, shrug your shoulders and tell yourself, *There is no use to try, this is the way life is now and it will never change,* you will never be motivated to get out of the ruins of the past and embrace the possibilities of a God-directed future.

Thoughts and Notes

Chapter 2

OBTAIN A VISION

I told no one what God had put into my heart to do at Jerusalem.

—Neh. 2:12

THE ONLY WAY to successfully rebuild your life, marriage, home, business or church is to have a vision or a desire put into your heart by God. Vision will give you the desire or drive that is needed to accomplish what is laid out before you.

I have dealt with both sides of this equation. I have worked with couples who were struggling in their relationship. If one of the partners did not want to work on the marriage, there was little that could be done to change that person's mind.

One couple came to see me after the wife had already left the home. The husband had been verbally abusive during the entire seven-year marriage, and she feared for her safety. When he began to abuse their daughter, it was the last straw. She was done with him. No matter what he promised to do or how much he promised to change, her decision would not be swayed. She no longer had any desire to make the marriage work. I told the man that as husbands, we are stewards of our families. We are responsible for their provision and care. He failed at his responsibility to do that.

Thankfully, it does not always end this way. There was another couple who was referred to me by a family in our church. I was their last stop on the way to a divorce. They were not sure if they even loved each other any more, but they both were willing to try to reconcile the relationship. That is the key! Once we were able to sort out the problems that were weighing them down, they were able to see their relationship and each other in a different light. They worked through their problems and are still together today.

In Nehemiah 2:12, Nehemiah says the following about the vision God had given to him: "I told no one." There will be times in our lives when we need to learn to keep quiet about what God has laid on our heart. Nehemiah's strategy was to tell no one about the plan God had given him concerning Jerusalem.

There are two reasons why this should be done. First, people may come against you before you have a chance to even get started. (We will examine this further in chapter 3). Second, no one will understand the vision but you. It is not for other people (right now); it is for you from God. You may have a heart to rebuild, but you do not have direction. In other words, God will need to provide a plan to get you from the ruins on the road to rebuilding.

A Season of Waiting

One of the hardest lessons we have to learn once we receive a vision from God is that there will often be a season of waiting. One of the mistakes people make when God drops something in their heart is thinking that it will be fulfilled within a day, a week or even months. For most of us, the process will take years before we see the fulfillment of what God has promised. Like Abraham and Sarah, we may be tempted to come up with our own plans during this time and operate outside of God's timetable. Abraham and Sarah's plans were wrong, and they failed. And so will yours.

In Genesis 37:5-10, God gave Joseph a vision of his family bowing before him. But God did not tell him how He was going to accomplish it. In fact, there are a number of things that God did not reveal to Joseph about how this vision would come to pass.

For instance, God did not tell him that he would be sold into slavery and go to Egypt. If God were to tell us what was going to happen on our way to fulfilling His purpose for our lives, most of us would tell Him, "No thanks. The process is too painful."

God did not tell Joseph that he would be falsely accused of making a pass at Potiphar's wife and go to prison. Joseph's position of authority in Potiphar's house could easily be understood as a fulfillment of the vision. The reason I say this is because at Potiphar's house Joseph had power, he was doing well, and things were looking up. It would have been easy for him to settle in at Potiphar's house and falsely assume that he had arrived at his destination. But God had greater plans for him.

God did not tell Joseph that he would be left in prison for two full years before He decided to get things moving along. Joseph asked the butler to remember him, but the man forgot. Joseph was trying to help God out and shortcut the process He had planned for him (see Gen. 41:1).

God did not tell Joseph that He would give him the interpretation to Pharaoh's dream. This would be the first step in the fulfillment of the vision. But only God could fulfill it. It was out of Joseph's hands.

Finally, God did not tell Joseph how long it would take for the vision to come to pass. More than 23 years elapsed from the time of Joseph's vision to the time that his father, Jacob, moved to Egypt!

Joseph is a perfect example of someone who had a dream from God and endured a season of waiting before that dream could become a reality. When God lays a vision on your heart, there is a process that must take place before you can begin the journey of fulfilling the promise. This is another reason why it is important not to tell people what God has told you: people count time. If you tell them what God has told you, they will pressure you and ask, "When will the vision take place?"

We can look back and see what God has done, but we must move forward by faith.

God Directs the Vision

We also must make sure that when we have a vision, it is God who is leading us, not our own imaginations or grandiose plans. In Judges 6, an angel appeared before Gideon and informed him that God had chosen him to defeat the Midianites, a tribe that had been oppressing the people of Israel. To ensure that God was going to be with him, Gideon requested a number of signs from the Lord.

First, he placed a fleece of wool on the threshing floor and requested that in the morning the fleece would be wet with dew while the ground around it was dry (see Judg. 6:36-40). God granted his request. Gideon, asking God not to be angry with him, then requested the Lord to make the fleece dry and the ground around it wet with dew. "And God did so that night. It was dry on the fleece only but there was dew on all the ground" (v. 40). This was Gideon's way of making sure that it was God who was directing his steps.

There are two points I need to make here. First, it is important to point out that God did not rebuke Gideon for making these requests. Gideon's faith was not challenged. God did not ask him why he did not believe Him when He answered the first request, let alone when he made the second one. In the same way, you should never believe that desiring to make sure you have truly heard from God indicates a lack of faith. You may not have a fleece, but there is always something you can bring before the Lord as a request for Him to answer so that you know you are going in the right direction.

Second, the vision cannot violate the Word of God. No matter what you believe God has spoken to you, He will not at any time ask you to act contrary to His Word. There have been, and still are, people who have led themselves, their families, their churches and their organizations into ruin because the vision they were following was not based on God's Word. A vision will promote God, not people.

Before the dream or vision becomes the focus of your life, you need to make sure that it is truly from God. Here are several ways you can discern if God has placed or dropped a vision in your heart:

1. God affirms that the vision is from Him. Put a fleece out before the Lord and pray, "God, if this is from You, please do this or that."
2. The dream does not violate the Word of God. Be sure to measure it against God's Word.
3. The vision is implanted or is birthed inside of your spirit. If the Lord has placed the vision down deep inside of you, He will unfold the plan and begin showing you the bigger picture.
4. The vision endures through time. God does not speak to you or drop a vision into your heart only to have it pass away two to three years down the road. That's a fad, not a vision. A vision will endure the test of time.
5. The vision motivates you. A vision has the ability to motivate you to action. The power of this motivation is amazing—God using ordinary people to do extraordinary things for the Kingdom. Vision is what God gives to you when no one else can see the potential in what seems to be an irreversible circumstance.

6. The vision requires sacrifice. There is a price to pay and a process to endure to see the fulfillment of the vision. The price that some pay in fulfilling what God has called them to is huge—leaving well-paying jobs to go into the ministry; selling everything they own to go to the mission field; leaving families and a well-established support system to go to a country where no one knows them. That is what a vision or a calling will do.

Remember, if God drops a dream or vision into your heart, you may not want to share it with others. They may not understand your goal. It did not make sense to the people that Noah should build an ark when it had never rained. Yet God gave Noah clear direction to build an ark. The goal that God has given you—the calling that is on your life—is between you and Him. The job He has for you has been shaped for your personality and gifts so that you can be used for what He has called you to do.

Once you have established that God has really placed something on your heart, the next step is to assess the impact it will make in your life. There are three important points to consider:

1. The vision will become the focal point of your life. This is important because whatever you are rebuilding will need your full attention.
2. This vision will dictate and give direction to your life. Every decision you make will be based on the vision that God gave you.

3. God will be responsible for fulfilling the vision. This is where so many people start out with the right motives but end in disaster. They believe that they are solely responsible for fulfilling the vision. Every step of the way, Nehemiah acknowledged how God had provided all he needed to get the job done. Some people have lost everything in the name of the Lord because they got ahead of God.

It is important to realize that when God places a vision into your heart, it will be the catalyst you need to make the necessary changes in your life—changes that must be made in order to accomplish what God's plans are for you. If your marriage is going to be put back together, there must be changes. If your business is going to be restored, your practices must change. Your mindset and your thinking will need to be completely changed. We are talking about life-changing vision and purpose! The only way to rebuild your life and be completely healed is to go toward new beginnings and new horizons. Why? Because new beginnings bring a glimmer of hope where there was no hope before.

God Is at the Center of the Vision

There are still more nuggets to be gleaned from Nehemiah 2:12. Remember, God was the one responsible for placing the desire for rebuilding the wall around Jerusalem in Nehemiah's heart. If we are going to be used of God to rebuild anything in our lives, He must be in the center of it. Not only must He be the center of it, but He must also be the one responsible for giving us the plan and resources that will be needed to rebuild.

Nehemiah tells us that "God had put it in his heart." The word "put" here in Hebrew means "to turn the heart to something or to appoint or assign." This is very important in the healing process. If you are a pastor or leader at a church that has been deeply hurt, you have an assignment from God to be where you are for now. Your gifts and abilities are what God is going to use to bring healing, stability and vision to a hurting congregation.

At this point, the congregants probably think that none of these things can be accomplished. Once a church has gone through a difficult season, there will always be those who feel that God no longer wants anything to do with them. The people who are left will have questions on their minds such as, *What do we do next? Should we close the church doors? Who will come to our church now after all that has happened here?*

If you have been given the ministry of going into broken churches and putting them back together, these questions will be directed toward you. You will be viewed with suspicion. People will wonder why you came to their church and what your motive is for being there. The answer is that God sent you. As a pastor or leader, you can take comfort and find strength in knowing that God has assigned you to your current task. Assignments are given to those who are deemed capable of doing the job. You would not be there if God did not believe that you were ready for it and able to do it. Often, God's appointments or assignments are bigger than we are so He can draw our gifts out. The bigger the assignment, the more we lean on Him.

The second meaning of the word "put" is "to put anything into one's heart" (used if God is doing the placing). For you to commit to rebuild your marriage or business or to work through the area of your life that has been devastated, God has to be the one who places that desire on your heart. Without that desire, you will never take the steps that are needed to rebuild. This is the motivating factor that will keep you going during the rebuilding process.

As I have mentioned, if either spouse in a marriage relationship is not willing to make the relationship work, it will be doomed to fail. This is especially true if the spouses have been wounded by the conduct of their mates. The hurt and embarrassment of the failure that has taken place leaves them with little or no desire to make the marriage work. In my own experience, no matter what I have tried to do to help them, it always ends in divorce. The desire or motivation that is needed to work on their relationship is gone. One wife I counseled looked at me and simply said, "I have had enough. I am done."

This is also true if a spouse has no desire to change his or her destructive lifestyle—if the spouse enjoys the way he or she is living or does not believe what they have done is wrong. Unless God intervenes, this way of thinking means that he or she will never change. The spouse who has been wounded—perhaps based on the offending spouse's acknowledgment that he or she was wrong and promise to begin working at healing the hurts—may be willing to get help and try to make the relationship work. But if the spouse refuses to admit the guilt of his or her actions, there is no guarantee it will not happen again. This attitude makes it almost impossible to rebuild the marriage. The key element to building a marriage is trust. Once that element is missing, the foundation that is needed to rebuild is gone.

God Provides the Means of Accomplishing the Vision

In Nehemiah 2:12, Nehemiah uses the word, "heart," which means "intellect, to accomplish, to commit and to be industrious." It is evident from these definitions that there is a God-given plan. God impresses His plans and agenda into your mind.

Some would have you believe that you are simply led by the "Spirit," which is interpreted by some as being led by your emotions or the first thought that comes to your mind. To be led by the Spirit, however, means that it is God who is leading and directing your thinking. God gives you the plan and tells you how to accomplish the plan, and then you commit to the plan. This includes being industrious and using the means provided to accomplish the vision. If God has given you an assignment, He will provide all that will be needed to see it through.

You receive God's plan when the Holy Spirit impresses it on your mind. It may leap off the pages of the Bible. It may be the opening of a door that was closed before, allowing you to now step through. The point is that the Spirit needs to be the one who leads and directs you down the path of rebuilding and healing.

You will not rebuild any area of your life without a direction from God. Nor will you be completely healed from the wounds of the past unless God is the one doing the healing and the one providing the vision and motivation to move forward. This is especially important for pastors and church leaders. Do not attempt to bring healing and direction to a hurting church by the power of your own abilities or intellect. You must have vision from the Lord and a heart to want to tackle the work it takes to rebuild a church.

If God has opened the door for you to go to a group of hurting sheep, do not try to force something to happen. As a matter of fact, no direction may be the best direction to take! Love them, teach them and bring stability to the flock. They have already experienced enough change and turmoil. Let them catch their breath and calm down after what has taken place. They need to lie down by the still waters for a while. Hang in there, and at the right moment when God says they are ready to begin the journey, He will put the plan and the direction into your heart. (Note: If you are a pastor or church leader whose ministry is rebuilding broken and hurting churches, there is an outline in the appendix you can use to guide you and the congregation through the process.)

Thoughts and Notes

Chapter 3

DEAL WITH THE CRITICS

But it happened, when Sanballat heard that we were rebuilding the wall, that he was furious and very indignant, and mocked the Jews.

—Neh. 4:1

THERE WILL ALWAYS be Sanballats around who will not support your decision to rebuild. I am amazed at how critical and negative even Christians can be. There will be those who do not believe you should try to make your marriage work, rebuild your business that has collapsed, or try to breathe life into a church that has split or whose attendance has dwindled to only a handful of believers.

For instance, Sanballats will be there when you try to rebuild your marriage, reminding you of what you did wrong and how great your spouse must be to forgive you. I have heard statements from people such as, "You know, if my wife did that to me, I would never try to work our marriage out." Or, "If my husband treated me that way, I would not stay with him."

As a pastor, I have walked with people through all of these experiences and more. If you are experiencing a crisis in your life, the last thing you need are people judging and attacking the decisions you are making. If you have made up your mind to rebuild, you do not need people who will tell you why you should not.

Some people who are going through difficult circumstances seem compelled to tell everyone and anyone who will listen to their story. For the people sharing their struggle, it is therapeutic. Doing this, however, leaves them vulnerable to criticism and gossip, because when they tell others about their problems, they open themselves to the opinion of others. Rarely do others feel that they do not have the right to give advice and pass judgment on what has been said to them.

When opening yourself up to people, two things happen. First, people interpret your openness as permission to give their thoughts about why you are in the mess you are in. Second, people may have a sense that they are being asked to fix the problem, when all that was really needed was for them to simply listen.

Going hand in hand with criticism is gossip. When you tell too many people about what you are going through, it most likely will be told to someone else who is not even connected with the situation. By the time it comes back around to you (and it will), you will not recognize your own problem.

I advise people to not seek advice or support outside of the circle of friends who care about them and have their best interests in mind. This circle should be made up of only four to seven people. They must be mature, godly people who can give them honest input and insight—people who they will listen to and respect. This will allow them to have a covering and be accountable.

A support group is important when you are rebuilding your life because there will always be Sanballats there to remind you that it is your second, third or even fourth attempt. You will hear statements such as, "Why haven't you learned your lesson?" "No one is interested in what you are producing," "Do you want to fail again?" "Why embarrass yourself and your family with more failure?" or "Don't you remember what happened last time?" Yet there is something in your heart that leads you to try again.

Rebuilding a Church

In chapter 2, I discussed the importance of having a vision or desire placed in your heart. This is so important if your ministry or appointment is healing and rebuilding hurting and broken churches. This is one of the most difficult ministries into which someone can be called. I say this because my entire ministry has been going to broken churches. I have never received an opportunity to go to a church with normal problems. God has always sent me to churches that have significant and deep-rooted issues. From my experience, I have learned several important points about healing broken churches.

First, *you have to know that healing and rebuilding hurting churches is the ministry God has called you to do.* The circumstances that you are stepping into will never be pleasant. And to make matters worse, you did not create the mess, yet people will look to you for answers—even miracles. You have to remember that you are there because God laid a desire on your heart, not because it was the ideal church or the best move to make. As a matter of fact, the opposite would be true.

Second, *you need to realize that you will rarely stay long enough to enjoy the fruits of your labor.* Once the healing is done, God will most likely move you on to the next broken congregation that needs help. Someone else will step in, the church will blossom, and no one will remember that God used you to heal the church and lay the new foundation. You do not do this type of ministry to get credit or glory. If your ministry is healing hurting churches, you will most likely never be used to grow a church.

It can be frustrating when you have the heart, gifts and ability to be used of God in other areas of ministry but the door never seems to open. You watch as others go to bigger churches and other areas of ministry or positions, yet God never allows you to have that opportunity. But remember that men and women who are called of God to be church healers and restorers are rare people. Church rebuilding is not a limelight ministry, but the blessing that comes with it is that you get to help restore God's people to wholeness in their faith and walk with God. They will never move forward into a new beginning without your ministry.

Third, *when you leave a ministry and God moves you on, you must learn to leave the responsibility of that ministry in the hands of God.* Your job was to heal and lay the foundation for the rebuilding of the church. When that appointment is done, God will release you and turn it over to someone else. This is why it is so important not to leave a church or a ministry until you know that you have been completely released from it. In my own experience, I have found that God begins to deal with us about leaving a ministry a year before we are actually released.

This does not mean that you do not care about the people, ministry or what God may do there. It is just no longer your responsibility. This is difficult if the members of the congregation call you to complain about the person who followed you. There is nothing you can do about it—you must leave it in the hands of God. Turning a ministry over to someone else is hard, but hopefully the results will be positive and the next person will build on what you have started. However, sometimes that does not happen. In those instances, it can be difficult to hear that all of your work has been dismantled.

When you leave a ministry, the direction of that ministry will now be in the hands of God and the new leader or pastor. It will not be the direction that you were going, but you stepped aside, believing you had completed the task. When you resigned, you took off the mantle of leadership for that ministry. Remember that the man or woman who follows you has the right to hear from God and take the ministry in the direction that he or she believes God is leading.

Release it all to God and move on to your next assignment. When you arrive at that church, I guarantee that there will be at least one Sanballat waiting there for you. There will be someone wanting to know why you are coming there to rebuild the broken church. You will hear statements like, "Close the doors and let it die," "Let the people move on!" or "The church's reputation and name are too badly tarnished; it will never recover."

When you hear these statements, remember that after the church has split or the attendance has dwindled to nearly nothing, God only needs a remnant to perform a miracle. Sanballat will be there to discourage you and distract you from your appointment. He or she will try to make you lose the vision that God has given you for the ministry, but you need to stay focused on what God has called you to do.

On the Outside Looking In

Let's take a closer look at the verse for this chapter. Nehemiah's assignment was to rebuild the wall around the city of Jerusalem. But this simple plan upset some of the people in the area. "When Sanballat heard that we were rebuilding the wall…he was furious and very indignant and mocked the Jews."

This is the usual response by those who are not involved with the rebuilding process. Our sharpest critics are those on the outside looking in. They have not embraced the vision to rebuild. Not only have they not embraced the vision, but they also are actually against it.

The danger in only hearing about a plan is that people do not always understand the heart of the people to whom

God has spoken. I have had people come to me and make statements such as, "I heard they are going to try and reconcile their marriage," or "I heard they are going to try and rebuild the church," or "I heard they are going to restart their business." I do not allow these kinds of conversations to go on.

Sanballat was not only out of the loop of the rebuilding process, but he also became "furious" and very "indignant" with what he heard. The Hebrew meaning of the word "furious" here is "to burn or be kindled with anger." Can you imagine allowing yourself to become that angry over what someone else is doing? Not only was Sanballat furious, but we are told that he was also very *indignant*. The word means "to take offense, to vex anyone, to irritate or provoke." Sanballat had himself so worked up over the rebuilding of the wall that he was taking an offense over it.

There is not a lot known about Sanballat besides the fact that he was the leader of the Samaritans who were opposed to rebuilding the wall. There is no clear reason given in the Bible why he was against it. One of the tricks of the enemy is to get people upset over situations that really do not directly affect their lives. The rebuilding of the wall had nothing to do with Sanballat.

Not only was Sanballat against the rebuilding of the wall, but he also gathered others around who were likeminded. Look at Nehemiah 4:3: "Now Tobiah the Ammonite was beside him, and he said, 'Whatever they build, if even a fox goes on it, he will break down their stone wall.'" Sanballat found a man named Tobiah, and together they stood there and mocked Nehemiah and his colaborers as they worked on the wall. This is still true today. People get angry and oppose situations that really have nothing to do with them.

Combating the Sanballat Mentality

Being a Samaritan, Sanballat would have been a believer in the same God (Jehovah) as Nehemiah. Again, how often do we see fellow believers attacking other Christians? Yet Sanballat's opposition did not stop Nehemiah from obeying God and completing the assignment given to him: rebuilding the wall.

If you have a Sanballat mentality, there are two important points to remember:

1. *You need to mind your own business.* If a couple decides to work on their marriage, it is none of your business. If someone wants to make another attempt at rebuilding their business or a new pastor comes to a church with a vision and burden to rebuild it, it is not up to you whether the choices being made are right or wrong. That is between them and God. Unless you are invited to be part of the process, keep your opinion to yourself and mind your own business. Most of us have a hard enough time keeping our own lives straight, let alone worrying about what other people may be doing.
2. *You need to make it your business to be praying for them.* You need to lift up your brothers and sisters to the Lord. If a couple is struggling, pray for their marriage. God needs to intervene and heal their broken home. If people you know are struggling

> in their business, pray that God will lead in the rebuilding process. If God has directed someone to come to your church or a church in the area to bring healing and restoration, pray for the presence of the Holy Spirit to do a healing in the congregation. Regardless of the situation, the point is that we need to be praying, not judging.

There will always be Sanballats willing to give you an opinion of what you should or should not do. This is why it is so important to know where God is leading you. Habakkuk 2:2 says, "Write down your vision, make it plain on tablets, so you can run with it."

Get a journal or a notebook and write down the vision or the assignment that you have received from God. This will keep you on track and focused when the Sanballats come around to discourage you. It will encourage you when the rebuilding process is not going the way you thought it would. You must obey God's will for your life, not the opinions of others. Remember, most people do not know what God is doing in their lives, let alone what God is doing in yours.

Thoughts and Notes

Chapter 4

EXAMINE AND FORTIFY THE WALL

So we built the wall, an entire wall was joined together up to half its height, for the people had a mind to work.

—Neh. 4:6

DO NOT MISS the importance of this verse. It reminds us that rebuilding our lives is a step-by-step process. It has been my experience that after Satan has launched his attack and the dust begins to settle, people and congregations try to put the pieces of their lives or ministry back together exactly as it was before. It is human nature to try to bring normality to our lives after a season of difficulty or a devastating event. The fact is, however, that life is not normal and may never return to what we consider "normal" again.

There is no way we can experience life-altering events without those events permanently affecting our lives. And maybe they should. The truth is, if our "normal" lives were so great, why are we in the mess we are in today? In other words, for some of us, the status quo became comfortable and dangerous.

Rebuilding gives us an opportunity to examine each area of our lives for weaknesses. Nehemiah 4:7 states, "the walls of Jerusalem were being *restored* [repaired] and the gaps [breaks] were beginning to be *closed* [or stopped]." The rebuilding process was done from the ground up, stone by stone, one at a time. It had to be done this way in order to make sure that the wall was solid and secure. Where the breaks were, they were repaired. This verse uses the word "closed" or "stopped." The Hebrew meaning for the word is "to be stopped up." It is used to describe how the Israelites repaired the chinks of the wall.

Assess the Weaknesses

As we rebuild our lives, we need to closely examine what happened to bring us to this place. How did it happen? Why did it happen? What were our weakness? Where was the chink or opening that Satan exploited? I know people who will not admit their mistakes no matter how much time has gone by. When I meet with them, they never seem to have grown from the experience. But those who are committed to learning and growing from their mistakes will be able to admit their faults and then do everything possible to make sure that it does not happen again.

If we get into a hurry to get things back to normal, we may overlook or ignore the chinks. Rebuilding too quickly may cause us to miss an important aspect in the rebuilding process that may be the key to creating a solid future.

We are told in Nehemiah that the "entire wall was joined together up to half its height." There were no shortcuts in the process of repairing the wall. The entire wall was being rebuilt—not just part of the wall or the part where the wall was the weakest. The Israelites were rebuilding the entire wall. Even if there had been some areas of the wall that had not been destroyed, there would have been lines and cracks in what was left standing. The stress of the stones being pulled away from each other would have created weakness in the remaining stones. In the same way, when we are being stressed, it affects other areas of our lives.

Every facet of the wall had to be repaired, strengthened and evaluated for weaknesses. Each stone had to fit precisely. This was necessary to give it strength—the strength to withstand new attacks that would repel the enemy, provide safety and, most important, withstand the weight of the rest of the stones (burdens) that would be laid on it. It is the burdens or weight of day-to-day living that weakens our wall of protection.

Without exception, when people come to me for counseling, I find that it is never just one problem they are dealing with. During the course of the conversation, they often realize that there are many issues weighing them down. Life's issues, people, and Satan's plans will test the wall.

Maintain Vigilance Against the Adversary

First Peter 5:8 states, "Be sober, be vigilant, because your adversary the devil walks about like a roaring lion, seeking whom he may devour." Let's take a moment to examine the meaning of the Greek words in this verse. It will reveal to us how important it is to have a solid wall of protection.

"Be sober" means "to be calm and collected in spirit." This should be our response when life throws us a curve. We need to take a deep breath and let the Holy Spirit calm our spirit. This will allow us to think clearly and not make quick decisions or say something we will regret later.

"Be vigilant" means "to wake up from sleep, to give strict attention to and take heed unless through being remiss destruction overtake us." How many of the problems that we have faced have come because we neglected the warning signs from either the Holy Spirit or from people around us who tried to tell us that we were pursuing something that would end in disaster? We closed our hearts and minds to the warnings, telling ourselves that we were too smart to get caught, or that it was *only* a friendship, or that a certain person could be trusted with the accounts. Yet there was always that nagging feeling, prompted by the Holy Spirit, that the direction we were heading was not quite right.

In the end, we find that Satan has lured us into the trap he has laid for us. We have taken the bait and are now more involved than we thought we would be. Then the enemy pulls out all of the stops, and everything begins to unravel. By being remiss, destruction has overtaken us.

Why does Satan do this? Because he is our adversary. The word "adversary" means "an opponent in a lawsuit" or "an enemy." Without getting too theological, there are two conclusions that we can reach about why Satan is our adversary:

1. Every human being on planet Earth was made in the image of God, which qualifies us as an enemy of Satan, who is and always will be opposed to God and His creation. Whether Christian or non-Christian, each of us will have battles.
2. When we become Christians, we join forces with Satan's archenemy—God.

Notice the next part of 1 Peter 5:8: " your adversary the devil walks about like a roaring lion, seeking whom he may devour." The Greek meaning for "roaring lion" in this verse does not imply an old toothless lion, as some have tried to make it read. It means a young, fierce and hungry lion. I do not know about you, but the battles I have experienced have not been just a bunch of noise without any bite. They have hurt, and some have hurt deeply.

Notice that Satan "walks about." To "walk" means "to make do with opportunities." Satan is circling us looking for an opening, a weakness or a chink. So as we rebuild our lives, we must remember not to hurry the process, for we know that Satan will exploit this if we do. The last sentence of this verse tells us his goal. "Seeking whom he may devour." Satan is looking for someone to seize upon and devour.

Evaluate the Rebuilding Process

All of these truths are important reminders as we seek to rebuild our lives. This is why we must evaluate the rebuilding process. Every aspect of what has happened in our lives must be closely examined so that we will not repeat our mistakes. Many of those who experience a moral failure tend to repeat their failures. When their actions are first revealed, they are usually broken and repentant for what they have done. Then, a few months later, they find themselves repeating the same action. We need to acknowledge where there are areas of weakness and fortify them. There will be new attacks and new pressures to endure. If the first half of the wall is built correctly, it will be able to withstand the stress applied to it.

Allow me to make two points here. First, notice that Nehemiah did not try to build the wall all at once. He directed the Israelites to rebuild the wall one stone at a time. Building the wall to half its height showed progress and gave encouragement to the people of Jerusalem that something was being accomplished. This is the same mindset that is needed for us to work on our marriages, businesses, churches, or to build our own self-esteem. We should be thankful for the little steps that are being made.

Second, progressing slowly gave the Israelites an opportunity to inspect the wall for breaks and gaps. In the same way, we must look at the situation we are in and find the cracks in the wall that allowed the enemy the opportunity to come in. Was it greed that destroyed our business? A faction that split the church? A lust that caused the affair? If we attempt to rebuild too quickly, we may overlook the cause of the problem and not deal with it properly.

Avoid Being Lured from the Protective Covering

In James 1:14, we are given an insight to the importance of this process: "But each one is tempted when he is drawn away by his own desires and enticed." To be "tempted" means "to be enticed to do evil." Satan tempts everyone. The decision to act on the temptation rests solely on our shoulders. We are responsible and accountable for our conduct.

The next part of this verse reads, "When he is drawn away." The Greek gives us a hunting and fishing metaphor. The idea is that the game or prey is lured from its covering—"man is lured from the safety of self-restraint to sin." Can it be explained any better than that? Satan places the bait in front of us. The bait will always be our area of weakness. Satan will never go after our strengths; instead, he will place in front of us the temptation that will get our attention and, with time, weaken our resolve.

This bait is meant to lure us out from God's protective covering. Once we move out from under that covering, we are left unprotected and exposed to Satan's attacks. We take the bait and he reels us in. We do not set out to sin or fail but are slowly lured into it. We inch closer and closer to it. We circle it and maybe even touch it briefly. Our confidence that we will not be caught begins to build. Satan, like any hunter, patiently waits. Then, after we have toyed around with the bait long enough, we bite it. When that occurs, he has us.

The last few words of this verse are "of his own desires and enticed." The thought here is that the bait is something forbidden that creates a desire or that it is something for which we already desire. Either one is dangerous. We drop our guard and take the bait.

As you read this, maybe you are in the process of rebuilding because you "took the bait." Now is the time to inspect the wall for the area of weakness that Satan was able to exploit and begin to strengthen that area. It is easy to focus on the overall picture and forget that the little steps are just as important as the big project. Yet it's the little steps that will get you to the goal.

Thoughts and Notes

Chapter 5

RECOGNIZE THE STRATEGIES OF THE ENEMY

And I looked and arose and said to the nobles, the leaders and to the rest of the people, "Do not be afraid of them, remember the Lord, great and awesome, and fight for your brethren, your sons, your daughters, your wives, your houses."

—Neh. 4:14

WHEN NEHEMIAH MADE this statement to the people, the city still needed repairs. There are no verses that give us insight into the condition of the city of Jerusalem. It is also not clear how much of the city had already been repaired and what had yet to be finished. However, we do know that the city was underpopulated, because in Nehemiah 11 we are given an outline for re-settling the city.

The wall was not finished and the gates were not hung. In addition, Sanballat and others were mocking them and trying to sabotage the entire project. The people who were rebuilding the wall were under the stress of getting the project done and the fear of being attacked at any moment. Nehemiah was not declaring that God is great and awesome because of what He had done. He was declaring that God is great and awesome because of who He is. Although the job was only half-finished, Nehemiah did not let his circumstances dictate his relationship with God.

If you as a believer can grasp the depth and understanding of this principle, it will completely change the way you view your life. There is nothing that you and I can accomplish or achieve that makes God great; He already is! However, sometimes if we do not see instant results, we begin to doubt the vision God has given us. It is hard for us to say that God is great and awesome while we are looking at the ruins. At this point, the vision is bigger than what has been accomplished. We declare God's greatness after the work is done—after the vision is fulfilled, after the marriage is restored, after the business is rebuilt, after the healing is complete from years of abuse. Yet the truth is that God is great and awesome even in the middle of the ruins, in the middle of the battle, in the middle of the storm, in the middle of a life-threatening diagnosis. God is great and awesome no matter what our circumstances are.

If God's greatness is hinged on what we are experiencing, then we will be like a weed blowing in the wind. This is why so many believers are up and down in their walk with God. If things are going well and they are experiencing a season of blessing, then God is great. But if life is not going well, they wonder where God is. Being a Christian is not about us or our comfort. It is about God, His kingdom and where we fit into His plan—not how God fits into our plans.

You may be looking at your circumstances and telling yourself that the marriage is over, the business will never start again, the vision is dead, or the church will never recover. There are people who do not support you, nothing is going right, and you are thinking it is not worth it. *Do not quit now!* Get this into your heart and soul before you make any decisions: God is great and awesome in spite of your circumstances. He is worthy of your highest trust and praise.

If we look at our circumstances like Nehemiah, we can be in the middle of the ruins and say that God is great and awesome, regardless of whether it turns out in our favor or everything falls apart. The end result does not reflect on God's character or His ability to perform a miracle.

In Nehemiah 4:15, we are told that "God had brought their counsel to nothing." I want to focus on the Hebrew meaning of two key words. The first is "brought." This means to "break, void, frustrate or bring to nothing." The second is the word "counsel." It means "to plan a purpose." Nehemiah was telling his followers that God is great because He had brought all the plans and purposes of their enemies to nothing.

Satan's Weapons

Isaiah 54:17 gives us another insight to the plans and purposes of the enemy: "No weapon formed against you shall prosper." The weapon is the source of the attack. Satan is the source, and he has many weapons in his arsenal to use against us.

First, he uses *spiritual discouragement*. This comes in the form of oppression, depression and discouragement. Satan drops thoughts into our minds to bring us down. This is especially effective in our result-driven society. If we do not see things happening the way we believe they should, we give Satan a perfect opportunity to discourage us.

Second, he uses *others to derail God's plans for our lives*. We have already established that Satan will use the Sanballats around the project site to discourage us, but he will also use those who are the closest to us. He tried to use the apostle Peter for this purpose. Not only was Peter one of the 12 disciples, but he was also included in Jesus' inner circle. When Jesus went to the top of the Mount of Transfiguration, Peter, James and John were chosen to accompany Him. When Jesus walked on the water, it was Peter who stepped out of the boat. When Jesus raised Jairus's daughter from the dead, the only one's He selected to go into the house was Peter, James and John.

In the Gospel of Mark, when Jesus asked His disciples, "Who do men say that I am?" Peter responded, "You are the Christ" (see Mark 8:29). However, when Jesus shared with them that He would be rejected and killed, and that on the third day He would rise from the dead, Peter "took Him aside and began to rebuke Him" (v. 32). Satan was trying to use Peter to talk Jesus out of following through with God's plan for the redemption for mankind. If he can't get the people on the outside to derail the plan, he will then try to find someone on the inside to do the job. Jesus' response is found in verse 33: "Get behind me Satan! For you are not mindful of the things of God, but of things of man."

There is no doubt that Peter's motives were good. He did not want Jesus to die. It is possible that the enemy can use the people closest to us to discourage us. Like Peter, they mean well, but they do not understand what God is doing.

The third weapon Satan uses is a *sense of exile*. This occurs when the events and circumstances that have taken place in our lives lead us to believe that we no longer belong or fit where we are. This sense of exile—of being in the wilderness—can take place for one of three reasons:

1. *People have literally turned against us.* Maybe we were voted out of a church or off of a church board. Or perhaps the satanic attack caused us to lose our job or to be removed from what we love doing. Now we are trying to find a new direction.
2. *Someone we depended on has passed away.* That person was our compass, our anchor, and now he or she is gone. This often happens when a spouse dies. All of the plans we made for the future are now gone. We have to rethink the direction our life is going and realize that that person will not be there to be a part of it.
3. *Something has happened to make us question God's presence in our life.* This is spiritual exile or wilderness—the sense that God has abandoned us. We go through the motions of reading our Bible, praying and going to church, but we do not sense

> His presence. We are disconnected from God and from people. This often happens after we have been wounded by someone or disappointed with God, or because something did not work out the way we thought. But faith says, "I do not have to see Him. I do not have to feel Him. *I know* that He is always with me."

Fourth, *Satan uses his own plans against us.* Satan unfolds a plan that has been designed to come against us and discourage us. He knows exactly what it will take to hurt us and bring us down. He knows what will make us worry. He knows what will tempt us and make us want to quit. These are the areas that he will target.

Satan is a deceiver whose instruments are evil. Get that into your thinking! He does not and will not play fair. He will use whatever and whomever he can to accomplish his evil purposes. He will use devices such as other people to discourage us or bring a temptation into our life that is almost too much for us to bear. He may launch an attack against our physical health or use the emotional stress of day-to-day living. He will use whatever he thinks will work to derail God's plan for our lives.

Now, there is one other point to consider. These plans are formulated in the realm of the invisible. This is why most attacks seem to come out of nowhere. Isaiah 54:17 says "No weapon formed against you shall prosper, And every tongue which rises against you in judgment You shall condemn. This is the heritage of the servants of the Lord, And their righteousness is from Me, Says the Lord." The word "formed" means to fashion a plan against us. It is the idea of a potter shaping clay. It is a plot that was fashioned or created to come against our weakness.

The promise of this verse is that "no weapon formed against you shall prosper." This means that the plan that has been launched will not succeed. It will not flourish. It will not accomplish what it was intended to do. When Satan launches a plan of attack against us, he has a desired outcome in mind. This verse promises that whatever that plan may be, God will intervene and short-circuit the plan. The plan will not be accomplished, and the satanic outcome will not be completed.

We see the proof of this when we look back on certain battles that we have experienced. If we really think about what has happened, we realize that it could have been worse. Remember, the promise here is not that God will stop the plan but that it will not succeed or come to its full-intended purpose.

Prepared Against Attack

Nehemiah 4:16 says, "So it was, from that time on, that half of my servants worked at construction, while the other half held the spears, the shields, the bows and wore armor, and the leaders were behind all the house of Judah."

Nehemiah divided his people into two groups. We are told that half did the building, while the other half waited at the ready for any attack that might take place. It has been established that Sanballat and others were against the idea of the Israelites rebuilding the wall. There was the possibility that at any time, the vocal threats could become a physical attack.

So, as we go through the process of rebuilding, we must put on the armor of God. In Ephesians 6:11, Paul tells us to put on the whole armor of God "that [we] may be able to withstand the wiles of the devil." The "wiles of the devil" are the plans and schemes that he sets against us. He is the author of cunning acts. We need the armor of God to protect us while we're in the middle of rebuilding and to protect us from the plans and schemes that are launched against us.

Verse 12 tells us whom we are wrestling with: "principalities, against powers, the rulers of the darkness of this age, against spiritual hosts of wickedness in heavenly places." These are the forces that want to tear our lives apart. Remember, we are rebuilding and defending ourselves at the same time. When necessary, we must fight.

I would like to share with you something that I have observed from my many years of pastoral ministry. A church is usually divided into two groups. Half the people in the church are workers, while the other half are prayer warriors. The workers enjoy physical labor and doing various projects in the church and around the church's property. If there is a church work day, you can count on them to be there. If you put a paintbrush or a hammer in their hand, they feel that they have accomplished something for the Lord. The members of the other group, the prayer warriors, are the ones who will come for a 6:00 A.M. prayer time in the church.

Rarely have I found a person who is involved in both groups. Actually, the people in these two groups tend to look down on each other. For instance, if we had a church work day, I would hear comments like, "Things would get done quicker if some of those from the prayer group would show up to help." And, of course, those in the prayer group would say things like, "You know, pastor, we would have revival in the church if those who are worried about the building would come to the prayer time."

The fact is that for a church to be growing, healthy and balanced, we need both groups. Neither group's burden or goals are more important than the other; they are just different. Half are building, and half are ready for war. There will be times that we are called on to do both.

Thoughts and Notes

Chapter 6

SECURE THE FOUNDATION AND EQUIP THE SWORD OF THE SPIRIT

Those who built on the wall, and those who carried burdens, loaded themselves so that with one hand they worked at construction and with the other held a weapon.

—Neh. 4:17

IN CHAPTER 3, I mentioned the importance of building a team of people around you who will support you as you rebuild. It is important not to try to rebuild alone. Without help, you will be doomed to fail. In this chapter, we will take this concept even further.

Nehemiah's strategy was to have two groups of people working on the rebuilding of the wall. One group was actually performing the repairing of the wall, while the other group carried the burdens (brought the building supplies to the builders). This emphasizes the importance of having a burden for what God has called you to do. Whether you are the one rebuilding or are the one helping someone else to rebuild, without a burden, you'll be unwilling to carry the load it takes to see the project through.

Like Nehemiah, when you are rebuilding, you will need people to support you. They must be people who care about you and what you are attempting to rebuild. They need to be people who will stand with you in the rebuilding of your marriage, your church, your business or your life. They must be people who will stand alongside you to encourage you, but also speak the truth when they think you are getting off track. Not only must they care about you, but they must also be *qualified* to help you. When selecting others to help you, you must make sure that they have the ability to be a vital part of the process. These are the ones who will be helping you to lay the stones and rebuild your walls and who will be responsible for supplying you with what is needed to complete the task. So they need to have the proper qualifications.

Your support system could take the form of a pastor, a trained or credible counselor, or a mature believer who has been seasoned from life's battles and has godly wisdom. Self-help books, seminars or other materials are also useful. Most likely, it will be a combination of some or all of these possibilities.

The Stones in the Foundation

As you begin the rebuilding process, it is important that you set the correct "stones" in the foundation in the correct order. Here are the stones you need to select to ensure that your walls will not come crumbling down:

The Stone of Prayer

First, you should pray for wisdom to select the correct people to be your team. Saturate the entire process with prayer. Ask God to give you direction on how to begin and end the process that you are entering. Prayer brings in all of the elements needed. God's Holy Spirit, power and authority are available to all believers. Prayer will pull your rebuilding team together and keep it together when the going gets difficult.

The Stone of Wisdom

Next, you need to seek understanding of the problem at hand and the issues facing the rebuilding process. Some people have a God-given ability to see the answers to problems when no one else can. They can formulate a plan that will resolve the roadblocks that are in the way.

The Stone of Knowledge

After gaining insight into the issue at hand, you need to develop a functional, practical and feasible plan to accomplish your goal. You know what the problem is, but how do you go from knowing the problem to laying out a strategy for dealing with it? With any rebuilding plan, there must be a beginning of the journey, a roadmap along the way, and a destination or goal so that you know when the process is finished.

The Stone of Foresight

By "foresight," I do not mean that you guess about the future or gaze into a crystal ball, but rather that you consider possible outcomes as events play out in the rebuilding process. Nehemiah saw the possibility of an attack, so he warned the people working on the wall and armed them with weapons to defend themselves. He told them that when the trumpet sounded they should locate him, for he was their rallying point in case of attack. He positioned himself so that he could view the landscape and see the enemy approaching. This is a gift given to all leaders. No one had attacked them, but just in case they did, he had a plan.

Whether you are the leader and the one responsible for the rebuilding or you are the one who has lost everything, someone on your team needs to have foresight. You need someone who will be looking ahead for the possible attacks, snares, weaknesses or relapses that could hinder the rebuilding process or even bring it to a screeching halt.

The Stone of Caring

You will need to select people who will care about you and your situation. If you are the one helping someone else, you need to care about that person's soul and help him or her get back on track with his or her life. Of course, this does not necessarily involve approving of what has happened. You may be helping someone working through a moral failure. There is no way as a Christian that you could condone this kind of conduct or approve of what that person did—sin is wrong—but you can still care about them.

The Stone of Correction

The stone of correction involves receiving guidance on how you made mistakes. This comes from two sources. One is the Word of God. There is no way you can read the Word of God without it speaking correction into your life. It would take selective reading to miss the verses that speak to your sinful nature and how to deal with the flesh. Correction also comes from those on your rebuilding team who have permission to speak a word of correction into your life when needed. This will keep you on the right path to full recovery.

The Stone of Honesty

After examining your situation, you need to be honest with yourself about where you are in the rebuilding process. What kind of progress have you made since you began the journey? Have you secretly stumbled along the way? Allow those on your rebuilding team to ask you difficult questions. Let them give you an honest evaluation of how they view your progress, and provide them with honest answers so that you can complete the process of rebuilding. If you begin to lie to your team, you are already destined to fail.

The Stone of Accountability

You must hold yourself responsible for your actions to God and His Word and to yourself as a man or woman of integrity. You must also be accountable to your team and to the standards or plans that have been established as guidelines for the rebuilding process. I have yet to see anyone successfully rebuild his or her life without being accountable to someone. The temptation will be to try and go it alone or to not put the effort into the process that is needed to achieve victory.

The Stone of Help

This involves getting support for your rebuilding efforts through books, seminars and other resources that will help you on your journey. Nehemiah 4:17 states that the workers "loaded themselves so that with one hand they worked at construction and with the other held a weapon." See how important it is to position yourself not only to build but also to be ready to fight? Nehemiah's team did both; so must your team. Building the wall and carrying the load was done in such a way that if needed, the work could stop. The Israelites could lay down their load to reach for their weapons and do battle with the enemy.

Although this strategy could have caused the project to move along at a slower pace, it was a wise way to do it. The work still got done, and the strategy created a sense of safety for those involved with the rebuilding project. Regardless of the reason you are rebuilding, you cannot do it properly if you do not do it in a safe and trusted environment. By a safe environment, I mean:

1. Safety in receiving and giving input without being attacked by others.
2. Safety that if at some point in the process there is a setback or failure, those around you will help you get back on track. This is not approval of a failure

but an acknowledgment that it may happen and that if it does, you will have the support to continue to rebuild.

3. Safety when those on the outside looking in want to attack what you are doing or judge the motive behind it.

The Sword of the Spirit

Nehemiah 4:18 says, "Every one of the builders had his sword girded at his side as he built." Satan's arsenal of weapons that he uses against God's people is endless. As a matter of fact, you are rebuilding as a result of a satanic storehouse of tricks, weapons or diseases that he has used to invade your life.

It was necessary for Nehemiah to have each builder have his sword on his side, ready for battle if need be. A sword has two purposes: (1) to protect and defend you against an attack, and (2) to help you advance in the battle against the enemy. Advancement is part of the healing and rebuilding process. As you make strides in the rebuilding process, you will grow stronger in faith. Confidence in God and in yourself will then give you the strength needed to complete the journey. Neither of these two options is possible unless you have a thorough and working knowledge of the weapon you are going to use.

In Ephesians 6, Paul describes the importance of the armor of God and how to use it. Notice what he says about the sword: "the sword of the Spirit, which is the Word of God" (v. 17). The sword, the Word of God, is a weapon of war. Paul makes it clear that we are in a day-to-day spiritual battle.

The word "sword" has several implications. First, "to bear the sword" is used of the one to whom the sword has been committed. We bear the King's sword. We have been given the Word of God. Not only are we to bear it (carry it, lift it up); we are also to use it. The authority of the Word of God belongs to us.

There are those who have abused this concept, claiming and declaring things in the name of the Lord that are nothing more than selfish motives. On the other hand, there are those who relegate the Word of God to simply an antique book. There are ministers who step behind pulpits who believe that the authority of the Word is not for people today.

Second, the sword contains the power of life and death. The Word of God brings life. It is through this power that the bondage of sin is broken. Bodies are healed. Salvation comes to a repentant heart. Where there is darkness, it brings light and life. Yet the Word also brings death—death to our old sinful nature, death to our flesh that needs to be crucified, all of which we would be powerless to do on our own.

Third, the sword is used for quelling wars, quarrels and dissentions that would destroy peace. You can use the Word of God to bring peace to a situation full of turmoil. How often have you prayed and asked God to go before you as you stepped into a difficult situation? When you arrived, God had already been there, and the entire spirit of the conflict changed. When Satan sets into motion plans that cause dissention and tries to destroy the harmony that is needed to rebuild, use the sword of the Word.

Fourth, the sword of the Spirit subdues the impulse to sin and proves its power and efficiency. This is a very important aspect of the Word of God for those who are rebuilding because of a moral failure. The power of temptation can be overcome. Satan will come at your area of weakness again and again. Unless there is complete victory over it, the temptation can be too much. What a powerful hope we have in God's Word.

The Rallying Point

With the people armed and ready for anything that could come their way, Nehemiah positioned himself on the wall so that he could see if or when the enemy was going to attack. Nehemiah 4:20 reads, "Therefore, whenever you hear the sound of the trumpet, rally to us there. Our God will fight for us." The blast of the trumpet would signal that an attack was under way.

If you are helping others rebuild their lives, you need to understand that you are the rallying point. They need to know that you will be looking out for the enemy during the rebuilding project. They need to know that if the enemy attacks, you will defend them, protect them and fight alongside of them.

Thoughts and Notes

Chapter 7

PLACE THE FOCUS BACK ON THE WORD OF GOD

Then [Ezra] read from [the book of the Law]
—Neh. 8:3

THE PEOPLE OF Jerusalem and the surrounding area had gathered in an open square to hear Ezra, the priest, read from the Word of God. In the middle of the battle, in the middle of the struggle, in the middle of rebuilding, we often put our focus on the problem and not on God. It is human nature for us to analyze what we are experiencing. We go over and over the events that have taken place—the events that have brought us to where we are today. We ask ourselves questions such as, *Why am I going through this? Why didn't God intervene and prevent this calamity? Why is God allowing this to happen? What did I do to cause this? I am innocent.*

We try to find the reason or cause for why we are going through this storm. If only God would tell us what He is trying to accomplish, then we could deal with what has happened. If only we knew the reason or the purpose, we could make the necessary changes needed to bring our suffering to a close. We want to make sense of the events that seem senseless.

These mind-numbing, mental gymnastics of searching for answers will cause us to get our eyes off the Lord and on our storm. Obviously, if our lives have fallen apart because of our own conduct, then we fully understand what has happened and why. However, that does not make what we are experiencing any less painful or our search for healing any less important.

The Storms of Life

For centuries, the apostle Peter has been used as an example of a person who took his eyes off of Jesus when he attempted to walk on the water. Matthew 14:22-30 gives us the description of that event.

Jesus had finished feeding the 5,000 who had been listening to Him teach that day, and the disciples had been sent to the other side of the lake. What was supposed to be a cruise across the lake quickly turned into a crisis when a storm arose that even the most seasoned fishermen of the 12 disciples could not handle. Isn't that how life can be at times? What we thought was going to be a simple plan goes from smooth sailing to a tumultuous ordeal.

The boat was about 600 feet from the shore, but the waves and wind prevented the disciples from completing their journey. Then, between the hours of 3:00 and 6:00 in the morning, Jesus came walking across the water to them.

They became fearful, believing they were seeing a ghost. Jesus spoke to them and told them to "take courage, it is I, do not be afraid" (v. 27). Then Peter said, "Lord, if it is you, command me to come to you on the water" (v. 28). Jesus told him to come. So Peter stepped out of the boat and walked on the water toward Jesus.

But then, "*seeing the wind*, he became *afraid,* and beginning to sink, he cried out saying, 'Lord save me'" (v. 30, emphasis added). No matter how mature or seasoned we are as believers, the storms of life can and will cause us to take our eyes off Jesus. Peter saw the wind and waves. He could feel the rain in his face. The storm got his attention. Once that happened, he became afraid and began to sink.

Matthew 14:31 says, "Immediately Jesus stretched out His hand and caught him, and said to him, 'O you of little faith, why did you doubt?'" Jesus stretched out His hand to save Peter. He is stretching out His hand to us. Regardless of whether what has happened is our fault or is the scheming of the enemy, when we start to sink, Jesus is always there to help us. Jesus asked Peter, "Why did you doubt?" His faith wavered because of the storm.

The Problem with Blame

If I asked you the question, "What are you going through right now?" or, "Who has hurt you?" I would venture to guess that you would be able to give me in detail the events that brought you to where you are today. You could give me the latest diagnosis, the reason your company folded up, the date your spouse walked out on you. These are the events that will be etched into your memory for a lifetime.

The list could go on and on. The point is that during the storms of life, we often take our focus off of God and onto the storm we are facing. It is easy for us to place our attention on the wind and the waves and worry that we will sink. It is easy for us to place our focus on the people who have hurt us and are responsible for the situation we are currently in. Yet placing our focus on these areas or people will only create a spirit of blame.

The people of Jerusalem could point a finger directly at King Nebuchadnezzar and declare that he was the reason their lives were ruined. He was the reason their families were split up, their people were killed and led into captivity, their city walls were broken, and their gates were burned. It was all his fault. We may likewise point a finger at the source of our hurt, but the truth is that blame never brings healing.

The ability to blame someone or circumstances for our problems and troubles will give us psychological permission to remain in a wounded and bitter condition. If we can blame someone else for the circumstances we are in, we then take the responsibility off of ourselves for trying to change what has happened. Because we have someone or something else to blame, we can then feel sorry for ourselves and have a pity party for as long as we want.

I realize that I do not know how deeply you have been wounded or what has happened to you in your life's journey. The fact is that everyone has been deeply hurt by someone at sometime. Life has undoubtedly thrown circumstances at you that you were not prepared to handle. Join the human race! Or maybe you have been angry with God because He did not answer your prayers the way you wanted Him to. Maybe God did not deliver you from what you are experiencing. God did not stop the plans that were made when the people you were trusting rose up against you and stabbed you in the back. He did not heal a loved one of a disease that took his or her life or left him or her debilitated.

The fact is that when we hold anger and bitterness toward those who have hurt us, we only end up hurting ourselves. We know this is a true statement; nevertheless, we still do it. The truth is that Satan cannot ruin your life. He can only ruin your plans. If Christ is our life, He cannot be taken from us no matter what life throws our way.

Grounded in the Word

After you have been hurt, have you ever run into the person or persons who hurt you? Maybe they are laughing and joking, going about their business, acting as though what happened has not affected them at all. All the while, you remain mired in hurt and pity for yourself.

You need to realize that you will not get even with anyone by holding a grudge against that person. You may not be able to control what has happened to you or do anything about the people who have hurt you, but you can avoid using blame as an excuse to not change your attitude or be healed. It is time to get over what has taken place and get on with your life. This process will not take place without God's intervention or the Word. You will not get over being hurt without making an effort to do so.

Notice in the story in Nehemiah that Ezra read from the Word of God. God's Word will bring you the hope and strength you need to be able to walk through the healing process. You can trust and lean on it during the darkest times in your life. To conclude this chapter, I want to share six aspects of the Word of God with you.

1. *All promises are grounded in God's Word.* God does not and will not operate outside of His own Word. We can go through the Word of God and find all of His promises to us—the promises of healing, restoring, provision and help when we call upon Him. We can read verses that help heal the brokenhearted. We can stand on His Word for the hope and healing we need.
2. *God's Word promises that we will be with Him for eternity.* This to me is the greatest aspect of the Word. No matter what is happening in our lives or how our lives are turning out, when it is all over we will be home with the Lord. All that has happened will be insignificant when we see Him.
3. *God's Word has been uttered by the living voice of God.* Ponder the power of this statement. A living God uttering the living Word. The reason God's Word changes lives is because it is alive. Dead words do not bring salvation. Dead words do not bring restoration. Dead words will not give us a hope for the future. It only comes from the living and powerful Word of God.
4. *The truth of God's Word never wavers.* It is necessary for us to put faith in God's Word. The world around us is constantly changing what it believes. One

religion or philosophy becomes the new fad for the moment, and when that has been exhausted, people move on to the next wave of thought. Faith in God's Word does not waver, regardless of what is happening to us or around us. We must believe in God's Word with all of our heart, mind and soul.

5. *God's Word provides comfort.* There are countless passages of Scripture that will bring comfort in a time of loss or need. I realize that if you have recently experienced a loss, these words may seem empty compared to the pain you are going through. But as time goes by, the comfort and strength the Word provides will be there, waiting for you to discover.
6. *God's Word is powerful.* The Word of God can be used to rebuke the enemy and to take authority over temptation. It can be joined with faith and hope to accomplish God's will. It can correct, which is often not pleasant but necessary. Correction is done to shape the image of Christ in us.

For all of these reasons, placing your focus back on the Word of God is a must if you are going to rebuild your life.

Thoughts and Notes

Chapter 8

FORGIVE AND REPENT

The children of Israel were assembled with fasting, in sackcloth and dust on their heads...and they confessed their sins and iniquities of their fathers. They confessed and worshipped the Lord their God.

—Neh. 9:1-4

AT FIRST, IT would seem odd that the people of Israel needed to repent and fast. From what? If anyone could point a finger of blame at someone else for their circumstances, it would have been them. Nebuchadnezzar had destroyed their city, taken their family members captive, and ransacked the Temple of God. Why would the victims have to repent of their sins and the iniquities of their fathers?

There are four important insights we can gain from this story as to why we need to forgive those who have hurt us and seek forgiveness from those whom we have hurt.

1. Forgiveness Allows Us to Avoid a Victim's Mentality

The *Random House Dictionary* defines the word "victim" as "a person who suffers from a destructive or injurious action or agency." The situation and circumstances that you are in were most likely caused by the actions of other people. These could be the people who plotted against you at work and prevented your promotion, the board members who asked you to quietly resign from the church so that there would be no trouble, or the spouse who has acted in ways that have left you wondering what to do next. You may be completely innocent, yet the actions of others have ruined your life. You are helpless to stop what is happening to you because the powers affecting your life are mightier than you.

A victim is also defined as "a person who is deceived or cheated." How many times have you been led to believe that you were at the top of the next promotion list? Maybe someone took your ideas, tweaked them, and then presented them as their own in a board meeting. There was nothing you could do but sit and listen.

We have a friend in Nashville who related the following story to us. He is a worship leader of a church and, like most people who go to Nashville, is a singer and songwriter. He had written a song and presented it to someone that was supposed to take it to a recording company. A few months went by, and he had not heard from this agent. But he did hear his song played on a radio station. He was crushed. After contacting a lawyer, he found out that there was little he could do. He learned a very hard lesson.

People in the secular world and in the church world can and will do things that will hurt us. If we do not forgive those who have hurt us, we are destined to adopt a victim's mentality. We rationalize that because these people did something to us, we have the right to hold a grudge against them. The events that caused the pain are the first thing that comes to our minds when we wake in the morning and the last thing we think about when we go to sleep (if we can) at night. An unwillingness to forgive will steal our peace and our joy if we let it. A victim is one who not only has allowed the circumstances to control him or her but also has allowed the circumstances to win. This is far from living a victorious life in the Lord.

Everyone has been hurt by someone. Until you forgive those people, they will have control over you. If their name is mentioned or the circumstances that caused the pain are brought up, you will get sick to your stomach or feel your blood pressure begin to rise. But if you forgive them, which is a conscious act on your part, the healing process will begin. And remember, forgiving someone does not mean that you approve or accept what he or she did, or that you condone his or her conduct as acceptable or right. It was not.

In Nehemiah 6, we see that Sanballat and others were still trying to stop the rebuilding of the wall. They wanted to lure Nehemiah away from the worksite to a place where they could kill him. Nehemiah 6:5 tells us that five times Sanballat sent servants with letters to get Nehemiah away from the rebuilding of the wall. They even offered to meet at the Temple of God. False prophets were hired to try to deceive and frighten him. But in verse 14, we have Nehemiah's response to what was happening: "My God, remember Tobiah and Sanballat, according to these their works, and the prophetess Noadiah and the rest of the prophets who would have made me afraid."

Two points need to be made here. First, Nehemiah left the punishment and retribution for Tobiah and Sanballat's conduct to God. Romans 12:19 reads, "Beloved, do not avenge yourselves, but rather give place to wrath. For it is written 'vengeance is mine, I will repay,' says the Lord." The passage of Scripture is clear. We are *not* to get even with someone who has hurt us. This is so difficult to do. It is human nature for us to want to get even. Yet God says *no*! As a matter of fact, we are told that it is God who will determine if vengeance is necessary. If so, He will be the one who will perform it. The problem is that we do not believe He will do a good enough job—or maybe that He will not get even for us at all. We may believe that what was done to us deserves vengeance; however, it does not mean that God necessarily agrees.

Second, by leaving the punishment to God, Nehemiah was able to go about the business of rebuilding the wall. He did not go off somewhere and seethe over what had been done to him. Nor did he hold a grudge against those who wanted to kill him. His peace came by simply trusting God to take care of the situation. By doing this, he was able to avoid planting seeds that might have led to him adopting a victim's mentality.

Most of us say that we leave our hurts in God's hands, but few of us rarely let it go. Forgiveness is our opportunity to release what has happened and give it to God. Or maybe it was not people but uncontrolled circumstances that hurt us. We go to God seeking answers, but there are none, which makes the matter that much more difficult. Remember, Nehemiah did not try to find all the answers. He simply said, "Let God take care of it."

Praying for and through what has hurt you is not going to be a one-time act. You know as well as I do that the enemy will bring what has happened to your mind every day if he can. The process of healing can take months and, for some, even years. Do not stop the process; follow it through to victory. If you forgive those who have hurt you, the control and influence they have over you can and will be broken. You will be set free, and the healing that you have needed and longed for will take place. You will no longer be the victim but the victor.

2. Forgiving Others Will Prevent Us from Becoming Bitter, Angry and Resentful

Forgiveness will prevent us from becoming bitter. The dictionary defines "bitter" as "piercing or stinging, an intense hostility." Once we have been hurt, it is so easy to embrace the emotion of bitterness, which is a very short step to hate or hostility. Bitterness will take root deep in our soul, controlling our thoughts and feelings. It will affect our view of life. No matter how good things may be going for us, bitterness will cloud the view of the blessings that are in our lives.

Forgiveness will also prevent us from becoming angry at what was done to us. "Anger" is defined as "a strong feeling of displeasure and belligerence." Each of us can relate to the feelings of displeasure. I mean, who likes being hurt? This pain brings belligerence and defiance in our hearts and attitudes. This comes as a two-edged sword: On the positive side, we put up a protective wall so that we can manage the pain and not let anyone hurt us like that again; on the negative side, when the wall goes up, we no longer allow in anyone who could help us—maybe not even God.

In addition, forgiveness will prevent us from feeling resentment over what we have lost. To be resentful means to "feel or show bitterness or indignation." Indignation is a strong displeasure at something unworthy or unjust. When the events that shake our world seem so unjust and unfair, we cry out to God, "What have I done to cause this to happen to me?" It is when we cannot for any logical reason understand what has happened that this resentment settles into our soul. This is why those who have been hurt must repent of the emotions. This is so difficult, especially when they are the victims of someone else's scheme.

These negative and destructive emotions can easily become a part of our attitude, especially if we can justify them. Satan will seize every opportunity to remind us of how we were treated and that we have the right to feel the way we do. The reality is that when we choose to be angry, bitter and resentful, we are the ones in bondage. The person or persons who have hurt us most likely are not feeling anything.

I once had a speaking engagement at a church in Iowa. After I had finished the message, I took time to pray with those who desired prayer. There was a woman in her mid-sixties who patiently waited while we finished praying for everyone so that she could speak to me without interruption. She shared with me that the message had touched her. She said that not only did it minister to her, but also that God had used it to set her free from past hurts. I told her that I was glad to hear that. (I believe she wanted a more enthusiastic response.) She said, "You do not understand. God has set me free." I responded, "Great, tell me what happened."

She said, "As a child growing up, I hated my mother. She verbally abused me and continually cut me down. No matter what I tried or accomplished, she would find fault with it. I could do nothing right. Now, after 40 years of hating her, God set me free this morning." As we spoke, I discovered that her bitterness and anger toward her mother affected every relationship she had. It ruined her marriage and her relationship with her children.

Can you imagine carrying an offense against someone for 40 years and then having the poison of that bitterness infect every relationship in your life? If we are not completely healed, our bitterness will infect our relationships in our family, among our coworkers, and in our church relationships. What a waste of a person's life, time and brainpower!

The woman's mother was now dead, so she could not go to her and make the relationship right. But she did have to forgive her so that she could be completely healed and set free. That Sunday morning was the beginning of her journey. Her next move was to try and restore the broken relationship with her children and others.

3. Forgiveness Allows True Rebuilding to Take Place

We cannot put our lives back together unless we completely forgive those who are responsible for hurting us. I have met people who have been deeply hurt and mistakenly believed that trying to ignore what took place would somehow eventually bring healing.

Suppose someone was hurt five years ago. Instead of forgiving the person who hurt him or her, over time, he or she learned to bury it. The thought is, *Because I do not think about what happened as much as I did before, I must have dealt with it. I am doing better.* If this is the case, it is not forgiving others—it is just burying the pain. We must openly deal with what has taken place and admit that we were hurt, or that we made a poor decision, or that it is our fault that things fell apart. We must be honest about what has happened if we are going to experience real forgiveness.

If we try to rebuild our lives without forgiving those who have hurt us, the foundation we are using to rebuild our lives is weak and could crumble at any time.

4. Seeking Forgiveness Enables Us to Learn from Our Mistakes and Get on with Life

Maybe you are not the victim but the guilty party. Your conduct was what caused the pain or hurt in the lives of the people around you. Was it your stubbornness and pride that caused the church members to choose sides and split the church? Can the company's losses be directly placed on your shoulders? In other words, are you the one responsible for what has happened and where you find yourself today?

At the other end of the spectrum, maybe you did not step up and hold those around you accountable for their actions. You should have asked deeper questions when you became suspicious. "Where have you been? Where are you going? How long will you be? Who will you be with? How can I reach you? Can I accompany you? Why are you treating me differently?" You knew that something was not right; that something had changed in the relationships with the people around you. Looking back, you now realize that you should have said something, but you kept silent.

If the Holy Spirit reveals an area in which you could have done more or where you may have failed, repent and ask God to forgive you. Learn from your mistakes and get on with your life.

In Nehemiah 9:3, we are told that the Israelites confessed and worshipped. These two words are the cornerstone of rebuilding and healing. There are three Hebrew meanings for the word "confessed":

1. "To confess concerning oneself." You repent of your attitudes toward the people who hurt you. You confess the bitterness, anger and resentment, giving it all to God, and are set free from the bondage that has a stifling grip on your life.
2. "To show oneself as guilty." You accept responsibility for your sins and failures, and then ask God to forgive you of them.

3. "To praise, to celebrate." Thanksgiving and praise naturally follow the acknowledgment of benefits received. I have had the privilege of praying with many people over the years. Once they have confessed their sins and their consciences have been cleared, you can see the change take place in their lives. There is something very powerful about having our sins forgiven. Some of us may laugh, some of us may weep, and others of us may just bask in God's forgiving love and presence.

Worship is the result of having our sins forgiven. It means "to honor God with our prayers." When we experience this kind of forgiveness, we offer up prayers of thanksgiving to God for what He has done. Some may worship Him in song and praises. Worship also means "to submit oneself." Once we have experienced this kind of forgiveness and power, we submit our lives to God's way and His Word.

Once the people of Jerusalem had repented, they were then set free to worship God. Let it set you free from the past. Receive His forgiveness and grace. Then, with a heart that is full, worship and magnify the Lord your God.

Thoughts and Notes

Chapter 9

EXPERIENCE BREAKTHROUGH

Now at the dedication of the wall of Jerusalem, they sought out the Levites in all their places, to bring them to Jerusalem to celebrate the dedication with gladness, both with thanksgiving and singing, with cymbals and stringed instruments and harps.

—Neh. 12:27

THE REBUILDING IS done. Now it is time to celebrate and give God the glory. What began as an impossible journey of recovery and healing is now finished. The pieces of your life have successfully been placed back together. The pain and embarrassment are behind you. The plans of the devil and his demonic forces have crumbled. The Sanballats have been silenced. Those who doubted that something could come from the mess you were in have seen the hand of God perform a miracle. With God's strength, you were able to go through the rebuilding process and see it through to its finish.

Nehemiah 6:15 tells us that the wall "was finished on the twenty-fifth day of Elul, in fifty-two days." There will come a time when the rebuilding process will be complete and when what has happened in your life will no longer consume your thoughts every minute of the day. You will never forget what you have gone through, but you will be able to go on with your life with a new beginning and a new hope.

Nehemiah 6:16 states, "And it happened, when all our enemies heard of it, and all the nations around us saw these things, they were very disheartened in their own eyes, for they perceived that this work was done by our God." When God brings the pieces of your life back together, it will be a witness to all the people around you. People took note when things began to fall apart in your life. They will also notice when God faithfully puts those things back together.

Sadly, there are those who want others to fail. They will place roadblocks in their path to prevent their promotion. For instance, there are some pastors who hope for the failure of another pastor so that they will not have any competition. Not only does this hurt the lives of the people targeted, but it also hinders God's plan for the lives of the people they would have touched.

Nehemiah says that when such people see your success, they will become disheartened. Why? The answer is found in the next sentence: "For they [your enemies] perceived that this work was done by our God." God will cause your enemies to know that He is with you. And as long as God is with you, their plans are destined to fail.

God's Anointing

When things began to fall apart, perhaps you did not know whether you were going to survive or not. Maybe you did not care if you survived or even lived. Rebuilding was not a thought. But somewhere in the aftermath of the devastation, the Spirit of God began to move on you to rebuild your life. That was a breakthrough! By God's strength and grace, He provided the breakthrough you needed.

In 2 Samuel 5:17-25, King David believed that God would give him a breakthrough regarding his enemies. I find it interesting that even though David had two opportunities to kill Saul and become king, he chose not to do so. David did not try to get ahead of God's plan for his life by killing Saul. Instead, he waited for God's timing. He may not have respected Saul's conduct (who could have?), but he did respect the fact that God had made Saul king.

When King Saul died, David was anointed the new king of Israel. Second Samuel 5:17 tells us that the Philistines "heard they had anointed David king over Israel, and all the Philistines went up to search for David." The Philistines were not searching for David to congratulate him on his new position—they wanted to kill him. They represented a form of testing in David's life. When most of us receive a promotion or some other success, there will be those who will come to test us. We have to remember that when God anoints us, there will be those who will try to stop us—or at least offer resistance.

The word "anoint" in Hebrew has three meanings. First, it means "to shield." With God's anointing comes God's protection. I realize that we may experience some very difficult times as we journey through life and may even question God's promise of protection. However, we need to remember that God's protection is twofold. First, He gives us physical, mental and emotional protection during those seasons of hardship. God's hand may have been on us without us realizing it. How many times have we looked back later and wondered, *How did I get through that?* It was God's shield of protection. Second, God protects our souls. It could have been that we were slipping away from Him. The difficulties we experienced could have been God's way of bringing us back to Him. That is God protecting our soul.

A second meaning of the word "anoint" is "a vessel consecrated to God." God has placed His hand on our lives. We have been set apart to do the work that He has called us to do.

Third, "anoint" means "used of God in a future time or place." David was anointed to be the next king of Israel when he was a teenager, but he did not become king until he was 30 years of age. He waited 13 to 15 years before he became king. God may have anointed you today, but He may not use you for many years to come. You may wonder why. Just like David, there is always a season of preparation before God uses you.

The Master of Breakthrough

In 2 Samuel 5:18, the Philistines gathered at the Valley of Rephaim. I point this out because the Hebrew meaning for the word Rephaim is "the valley of descendants of the giants." David had done that before! He had faced giants and triumphed.

In verse 19, "David inquired of the Lord." He wanted to know if he should go up against the Philistines and, if he did, if God would go with him. God's response to David was, "Go up, for I will doubtless deliver the Philistines into your hand."

Notice that before David went into battle, he did three things. First, he asked God what to do. Second, he asked God if He would be with him. Third, he inquired as to whether he was going to be victorious. These are three important points to remember when we are believing God for a breakthrough.

Verse 20 tells us that David defeated his enemies. He declared, "The Lord has broken through my enemies before me like a breakthrough of water." He calls the name of the place Baal Perazim. The Hebrew meaning of this phrase is the "Lord or God of the breakthrough" or "the master of the breakthrough."

If you need a breakthrough, go to the Master of the Breakthrough. God has a plan for you so that you can break through the battles. He wants you to be able to break through the barriers that are preventing you from rebuilding your life. He is the God of the breakthrough!

Seek the Lord's Plan in Each Situation

The Israelites' victory was so overwhelming that the Philistines left (or dropped while fleeing) the images of the gods they took into battle. In 2 Samuel 5:21, David and his men picked up the battlefield littered with these gods and carried them away, most likely for the gold and silver they contained.

In verse 22, we read that "the Philistines went up once again and deployed themselves in the Valley of Rephaim." This really is amazing. Instead of acknowledging they had been defeated, one brilliant general decided to regroup and attack again. Is that not like the enemy? If one plan does not work, he regroups his forces and attacks again.

Verses 23 and 24 state, "Therefore David inquired of the Lord, and He said, 'You shall not go up; circle around behind them, come upon them in front of the mulberry trees. And it shall be, when you hear the sound of marching in the top of the mulberry trees, then you shall advance quickly. For then the Lord will go before you to strike the camp of the Philistines.'"

There is a very important insight that I must point out concerning these verses: David inquired of the Lord again. He could have easily thought to himself (especially after just experiencing a victory) that God would do the same thing He did before in the same situation. But instead, David decided to again seek out the will of the Lord. How many churches and believers are living in past victories, thinking that God won't change the plan? They do not even inquire of the Lord to see if He has a new plan for them.

By inquiring of the Lord, David learned that God had a different strategy for this battle. Previously, God had told him that He would go up against the Philistines *with* him and deliver them into his hand. This time, God said He would go *before* him into battle. The second plan was better than the first. I love it when God goes with me, but going before me is even better!

Can you see King David explaining this second plan to his commanders? "OK, guys, I have heard from God, and the plan is that we wait until we hear marching in the top of the mulberry trees." Surely he must have drawn a few strange looks from his generals. I mean, how often do you hear marching in the top of trees? But we must understand that while they were waiting, God was instructing the captain of His armies to have the heavenly hosts march on the tops of the mulberry trees. God had made a promise to His servant David that when he heard those steps, He would be going before him. What a promise! The Lord went before him and "did strike the camp of the Philistines."

Follow God's Plan

I believe verse 25 is the key to any breakthrough: "David did so as the Lord commanded him." David prayed and asked God for a plan, and God gave him the plan for victory. David did not take liberties with God's instruction by tweaking it for personal reasons or gain. He did not adjust the plan because he did not like it. He was obedient and did as God commanded.

Instead of getting a plan from God, too many believers get their own plan and then expect God to fulfill it. They become very disappointed when they discover that it is they who must obey God, not God who must obey them.

I want to reiterate that there will be a breakthrough at some point during the rebuilding process. This could be the moment your marriage begins to work out, or the moment the business recovers from bankruptcy and customers start returning, or the moment the church starts to show signs of life. It might occur when you begin trusting people again and come out of your shell, or when the depression that hampered your life for so long begins to lift, or when the turmoil in your soul slowly begins to calm. When breakthrough occurs, you will no longer be wrestling with God over what had happened or why He allowed it. The circumstances do not change, but you do.

Some people mistakenly believe that a breakthrough is only complete or valid if God restores everything that was lost. God is more concerned about your character and maturity than He is about what you possess. I have seen marriages fail to turn around and end in divorce, companies that never start up again, and churches that close down and put the building up for sale. When this happens, you take the lessons you have learned and do not repeat them.

A Time for Celebration

When the wall was finished, Nehemiah found people to celebrate with him. He found Levites, singers and instruments, and had a thanksgiving choir. He found people who would rejoice with him that the job was done. This could be you and your spouse celebrating the fact that your marriage will survive. Maybe it is you celebrating with a handful of employees as the business starts to produce again. It could be you gathering your church members and giving thanks to God for having favor on you. Maybe it means getting together with other family members to celebrate the life of a loved one who has died. Regardless of the situation, celebrate the breakthrough when it occurs and give thanks to God for coming out of the battle whole.

Thoughts and Notes

Chapter 10

THE END OF THE JOURNEY: GOD TURNS THE CURSE INTO A BLESSING

Because they had not met the children of Israel with bread and water, but hired Balaam against them to curse them. However, our God turned the curse into a blessing.

—Neh. 13:2

GOD IS THE only one who can use what the enemy has thrown at you and turn it around for good. He is the only one who can take your weaknesses and turn them into strengths. He can turn what Satan thought would be the nail in the coffin of your marriage, business, church or home into a rivet that holds these things together.

I know you are probably thinking, *How can God take a curse and turn it into a blessing?* To understand the curse that Nehemiah is talking about, we must examine the beginning sentence of this verse: "Because they did not meet the children of Israel with bread and water, but hired Balaam against them to curse them."

This is a reference to Numbers 22–24. The Israelites had just defeated the Canaanites and the Amorites and were camping on the plains of Moab. Balak, the son of the king of the Moabites, had seen what Israel had done to the Amorites. Numbers 22:3 says, "And Moab was exceedingly afraid of the people because they were many and Moab was sick with dread because of the children of Israel."

Instead of greeting the people of Israel with bread and water and welcoming them, Balak's fear motivated him to hire Balaam, a diviner, to curse Israel in the hopes of defeating them and driving them from the land. But the Spirit of the Lord prevented Balaam from pronouncing a curse upon Israel. No matter where Balak and Balaam went or what they tried to do to get around what God was doing, they could not. When Balaam went to curse Israel, it instead came out as a blessing.

Thus Nehemiah's statement, "However, our God turned the curse into a blessing." The Hebrew meaning of the word "turned" is "to overturn or to be overturned, to be overthrown." God takes the plans and schemes of the enemy and overturns them.

The Schemes of the Enemy Backfire

The book of Esther contains a well-known example of this. In Esther 3:5 we read, "When Haman saw that Mordecai did not bow or pay homage, Haman was filled with wrath." Haman was motivated by anger, pride and arrogance to kill Mordecai. Then, when he found out that Mordecai was a Jew, he wanted to kill all of the Jews.

So he began to put his plan into motion. Haman convinced King Ahasuerus that the Jews were the enemy of his kingdom. When Mordecai found out about the plan, he went to Esther and told her that she had to intervene on behalf of her people, or they would all be destroyed.

I want to stop here for just a moment. After more than 25 years of ministry, I can tell you that the Haman attitude is alive and well in the church today. There are always people who want to be "exalted" in their ministry, and they will become angry when the pastor does fulfill their wishes. I am not saying that they are not gifted. But it is not the gift; it is the attitude. These people believe that their ministry is more important than other ministries. Like Haman, they want everyone to bow down and pay homage to them. If you are a leader in any area of life, you know what I am talking about.

This happened to me in a church I pastored. There was a woman who just could not stand being out of the limelight or not having a position of power. I have always believed in mentoring and in people sharing ministry. However, because I would not give her the exclusive leadership in her area of ministry, or stroke her ego, she turned on me. I received a call one day from my superintendent asking me about some negative comments he had received from her against me. Then she began going around to the people in my church and tried to convince them that I was wrong and she was right. As the rumors started coming back to me, I found out that she was saying things to discredit me. Some of what she said were lies. Unable to resolve the issue, I had to ask this woman to leave the church.

During this season of attack, the Lord kept reassuring me to remember Haman and Mordecai. Haman was building gallows to hang Mordecai, but God turned the plans around. It was Haman who was hung on his own gallows, by his own plans. In the same way, this woman's plans backfired. The people she went to told her that they knew I would not have done the things she alleged. God can take the plans and schemes of the enemy and overturn them.

Satan will devise a scheme. He will try to put the people in place that he wants to use to fulfill his plans. He mistakenly believes that he is in control of the outcome and that his plan will succeed. Haman would not have been building the gallows if this was not his mindset.

It may seem that Satan has thrown something at you from which you cannot recover. You will not only recover, but God will also work on your behalf in the realm of the invisible to turn the enemy's plans around. You will bounce back—and maybe even end up in a place that was better than before. Where there had been brokenness that you thought would never heal, the Holy Spirit will come in as a balm and heal you from the plans that came against you.

Joseph's Remarkable Journey

The word "curse" means "to despise or bring contempt or to be shaken together." Satan despises your marriage, your church, your home, your business and your self-esteem, and he wants to destroy it. But God turns the curse into a blessing. He did it for Nehemiah, for Esther, and for Joseph. He will do it for you!

Joseph was 17 years old when he had two dreams. In the first dream, he saw sheaves of grain standing in a field. His sheaves were taller, and the others bowed down to it. In the second dream, he saw the sun and the moon and eleven stars bowing down to him. Joseph told his brothers about the dreams and said that they would bow down to him one day. Their jealousy caused them to plot together and find a way to get rid of him. But instead of killing him, they sold him into slavery, and he was taken to Egypt. There, he became the head of Potiphar's household. But when he refused to respond to Potiphar's wife's advances, she accused him of making a pass at her. Her allegations led to him being thrown into an Egyptian prison with no chance of parole.

Maybe you are reading this and can relate to Joseph's situation. Someone falsely accused you of something, and because you could not prove that the information was wrong, you lost your job or were removed from the church. Now there is a cloud of suspicion that seems to haunt you. It would appear that life could not get worse. But God has a plan.

In Joseph's cell were Pharaoh's butler and his baker. Both had dreams that they could not understand. They told Joseph the dreams, and he interpreted them correctly. Shortly thereafter the baker died, while the butler was restored to his original position.

Then Pharaoh had a dream, and none of his magicians or wise men could interpret it. In Genesis 41:13, we read that the butler remembered that there was a man in prison who interpreted his dream. So Joseph was taken from the prison and sent to the palace.

There, Pharaoh told Joseph that he had a dream that no one was able to interpret. Pharaoh dreamed that seven fat cows came out of the river, and while they were feeding, seven gaunt cows ate the seven good cows. In the second dream, he saw seven plump heads of grain spring up. Then, seven thin heads sprang up and devoured the plump ones. God gave Joseph the interpretation of the dream: there would be seven years of plenty followed by seven years of famine. Joseph was placed in charge of gathering enough grain to see Egypt through the difficult times that were ahead of them.

Genesis 42:1-2 reads, "When Jacob saw that there was grain in Egypt, Jacob said to his sons, 'Why do you look at one another; there is grain in Egypt, go down to that place and buy for us there, that we may live and not die.'" So the sons traveled to Egypt to buy food, little knowing that their younger brother Joe was now second in command over an entire country. To buy the grain from him, they would have to bow down when they met him. Joseph's dreams were now unfolding.

Joseph's brothers arrived in Egypt. He recognized them, but they did not recognize Joseph. In Genesis 45, Joseph finally revealed himself to his brothers, but told them not to be angry with themselves, because God had sent him before them to preserve their lives and preserve posterity. The brothers had sold him into slavery, but it was actually God who had brought him there. There is nothing like looking back over the events in our lives and seeing how God's hand guided our direction.

Joseph moved his entire family to be with him in Egypt. He also reunited with his father, whom he loved so dearly. And all because of a famine.

In Genesis 50, Jacob dies. Joseph's brothers were fearful that Joseph would now kill them for what they did to him. However, the truth is if he wanted to kill them, he could have done so when he first saw them. All he would have had to do was give the command to his guard, and they would have been dead or thrown into the very prison he had been in.

Joseph was told that his brothers were afraid of what he might do to them. Joseph's response is found in Genesis 50:20: "But as for you, you meant evil against me, but God meant it for good." There are three aspects of Joseph's response that must be pointed out:

1. *Joseph's response demonstrated maturity*. Joseph understood the bigger purpose that God had. When you have been sold into slavery by the ones who are supposed to love you, or when you are sitting in an Egyptian prison with no chance of ever being released, it is nearly impossible to see the big picture of what God is doing. I do not know anyone who is going through the trials of fire that can see past what he or she is experiencing, let alone the possibilities of what God will do when they have come out of the flames.

2. *Joseph's response demonstrated wisdom.* Joseph had the wisdom to understand that even though his brothers' motives were evil, God was able to turn those motives around for good. He even blessed and saved the brothers who had done these things to Joseph.
3. *Joseph's response shows that he had completely forgiven his brothers.* At any time, Joseph could have taken revenge out on his brothers for what they did to him. But he did not. As a matter of fact, he was crushed when he found out they feared him and thought he was just waiting until Jacob died so that he could kill them.

Some people do not have the maturity to forgive those who have hurt them, even if the situation eventually worked in their favor. Joseph may have been second in command of Egypt, and he could have become bitter about the journey that brought him there. But he did not.

The Blessings of God

Joseph never said that he enjoyed the journey. But he did know that God was in control of it. God took what was meant for evil and turned it into a blessing. The word "blessing" means:

1. "Favor of God that results in prosperity and good." When you see your life coming back together after what seemed to be the end, that is a blessing.

2. "Benefits and gifts from God." Christians become arrogant and prideful about the gifts they have received or the businesses they have built. Pastors begin to take credit for the size of their church. Nothing will make you realize that it all comes from God until it is all taken away from you. When God starts to restore it back to you, you will have a different attitude about who is the giver of the benefits and the gifts.

The blessing you experience after the curse is that you now have a stronger marriage than before, or that your business insights are better than ever, or that your skills at detecting a wolf in sheep's clothing in your church are sharper than before. Perhaps your leadership skills needed to be refined by the hand of God. Maybe, after years of abuse that had ruined your life, you needed to experience God's love and care and be set free. Maybe you needed to learn to love God even though you knew that at the end of your journey the outcome could not change, such as the death of a loved one. The blessing is that we love God not for what He can do for us but because of who He is.

The blessing could be that whatever weakness in your life had been exposed has now been strengthened. There is no doubt that as Nehemiah was rebuilding the wall, he did not just place the stones back on top of each other, but also repaired and strengthened any area of weakness that had been discovered.

The fact is that God can turn the curse into a blessing. Once you recognize this nugget of truth, it will help you get through the other seasons of difficulty that you may face in life. There is something to be gained by going through the experience.

Congratulations! You have completed the last step in the process. My desire is that the lessons you have learned from this book will have you well on your way to rebuilding your life, or will at least have given you a new hope and vision to help get you started. May the power and strength of God rest upon you as you rebuild.

Thoughts and Notes

Appendix

HEALING A HURTING CHURCH

THE FOLLOWING IS a guideline for the process of restoring a church that has experienced a season of difficulty.

1. Assess the Situation

First, consider what event has brought the church to its current situation. This could be:

A. Misconduct of the pastor, elder(s) or leaders.

B. Moral failure or abuse of the sheep.

C. Rebellious church leadership or people causing division in the church.

2. Assess the Damage

During this time of difficulty, remember that the people are hurting and have no direction. The programs of the church need to be evaluated for their effectiveness. Once this has been done, decisions can be made to strengthen them, streamline them or drop them. (Remember, these programs can be started again at a later date). In addition, the church facilities may have been neglected during this time. Be prepared to clean, scrub, paint and mow.

3. Congregational Response

Be prepared to bear some of the brunt of the anger and hurt. The congregation is most likely not upset with you, but with the circumstances in which they find themselves. There may be a lack of trust at first. It is important that the congregation know your heart and vision for the church. Expect an overreaction from the leaders and congregation, especially in response to what has happened. They may use the event as an opportunity to change things that they did not like about the previous leadership. Stay strong and on course, in love. You are the stabilizing factor.

4. Pastoral Response

Your attitude toward the previous leaders is very important. Do not be a part of any gossip or criticism. State the facts of what has taken place, but do not take part in attacking the person or people that caused the problems. If you do:

A. It will cause the wounds to stay open and fester.

B. It will lower your integrity and the integrity of your congregation.

C. It may prevent you from focusing on the present condition and from accomplishing anything constructive.

5. Reestablish Jesus as the Focus of the Church

Heal the hurts, build up the church and restore spiritual health, leading the congregants beyond their hurts without ignoring what has taken place. Set a new congregational goal and have a restoration service.

6. Begin Mentoring and Raising up Leaders

You can mentor and raise up leaders through:

A. Teaching and discipleship

B. Books

C. Videos

D. Seminars

7. Lead in Love and Strength

Pastor the church by leadership and discipleship, not dictatorship. Do not rush through the process. The complete healing of the church is critical for the proper foundation to be set for the future of the church.

LaVergne, TN USA
20 September 2010
197735LV00003B/187/P

9 781414 111940